What Readers Are Saying

"Peter Dziuban's book, *Simply Notice* is simply one of the best in the growing category of books leading us to our innermost nature as consciousness, awareness. Why? Because it offers a cornucopia of everyday life experiences, common to us all, wherein the direct experience of pure awareness or 'nonduality' is noticed, enlivened and lived, within and without. The results include greater harmony, inner peace, less reactivity, more stability and a deeper connection with one's self and the world. *Simply Notice* is a work I will turn to again and again."
—John Raatz, Principal, The Visioneering Group, and Founder, Global Alliance for Transformational Entertainment (GATE)

"Simply Noticing is like one big exercise in paying attention that is effortless and natural. And simple. The author persistently invites you to notice thoughts, feelings, sensations, objects, body, while leading you on an adventure of discovery of what you really are. To read this book is to experience it, which is a rare achievement for any work."
—Jerry Katz, Nonduality.com

"What Peter Dziuban does so eloquently in *Simply Notice* is to show that *Alive Presence* is what we really are, and that all that we think is real, is really an illusion, albeit an extremely convincing one. Through the logical pointers so carefully constructed by the author, you will definitely have the means to see through the illusion of a world of separate objects characterised by time, space, and fear. As an academic trying to lead my very educated audiences to see the truth of what's really going on, I most often fail. The illusion holds fast. With *Simply Notice* we now have a tool that should make the task of unmasking the unreal that much easier. This book is highly recommended."
—Professor Kriben Pillay, Dean of Teaching and Learning, College of Law and Management Studies, University of KwaZulu-Natal, Durban, South Africa

i

"If there was ever a step-by-step 'how to' book for releasing a body-based, thought limited reality, this is it. Peter Dziuban guides you on an experiential path awakening you to life's un-restrainable, infinite love---the love you are. This book is brilliant and perfect for those who may be new to spiritual literature. It's a fine accompaniment to his earlier *Consciousness Is All*."
–Sherry Harris, Psychotherapist, Spiritual Counselor

"*Simply Notice* is a wonderful, easy read. I felt like I was being communicated with, rather than being talked down to. Its simple style and poetic intelligence give the feeling of receiving a letter from a friend or loved one, inviting you to simply notice how marvelous you already are."
–Julian Christopher, Actor, Vancouver, BC

"What is it like to live happily, effortlessly, stress-free? Does it seem impossible or is it how Life really is? *Simply Notice* shows one the limitless nature of Life, free of struggle and full of joy. It helps you experience it, not just theorize about it. It's simply noticing what is already true. It's just gone un-noticed. You owe it to yourself to check it out. Enjoy!"
–I. Turner, CA

"Unless there's an emergency, stop everything right now and read this book! And be free!!"
–Jason Walters, Life Consultant, Phoenix, AZ jrwnow@ gmail.com

"In *Simply Notice,* Peter has put his finger on the heart of the matter for those desiring boundless freedom, peace and love. The simplicity, straight-forwardness, lack of spiritual jargon, and that the author shares from his direct experience make this book a must for any seeker whose desire is to awaken to the timeless Truth of their Being...which means to *Simply Notice* what you already are!"
–Michael Jeffreys, Awakening Blog: www.mjeffreys.com

"The Upanishads took shape when the ancient Maharishis taught millennia of years ago about 'Who you are and What this world is.' 'You are eternal, ever pure, unbound and wise Beingness; that's your true nature' was their unequivocal message. Peter is imparting that very Knowledge in simple and direct words with the same love and compassion as the ancient Sages in a style that is quite intimate and friendly. As he says early on in the book, 'This awareness is not some far off ethereal state that must be attained. It is this very awareness you are presently aware of being.' I have no doubt that Simply Notice would soon be the favorite modern day Upanishad for many a reader. It's a powerful, hands-on practical manual that equips us with tools that can transform our worldview. A sure-fire life-changer."
—Dr. Vemuri Ramesam, Author of Religion Demystified

"This book is a true gem! Whether you are new to spirituality -- or a seasoned traveler -- you will find every paragraph pauses you, yields fresh insights, even (or especially!) on a second or third reading. It is beautifully written and shines so brightly: more than anything else, it points you with unerring precision to the *softness* and *lightness* of the un-go-away-able Life that is reading this right now! I simply cannot recommend it highly enough."
—Colin Winborn, UK

"*Simply Notice* is simply the best. The Truth DOES set one free."
—Jim Crawford, San Diego, CA

"Instructions about awareness now come in many shapes and styles. Peter's often verge on poetry as he artfully softens the sharp edges of familiar words, crafting phrases that are nearly transparent to the light beyond them. He invites us to 'listen how silently the now goes about being present now'; to 'feel again how endlessly soft Love's gently alive presence is'; to notice the 'immeasurable quiet of Life's pure awareness.' It is his repeated invitations to simply notice our true self in these ways that make Peter's new book worthy of some of our precious time and attention."
—R.K. Grants Pass, Oregon

SIMPLY NOTICE

Book I

Clear Awareness Is the Key To Happiness, Love and Freedom

Peter Francis Dziuban

ISBN: 978-0-9986524-3-6 (sc)
ISBN: 978-0-9986524-4-3 (hc)
ISBN: 978-0-9986524-5-0 (e)

The author of this book does not dispense medical advice or prescribe the use
of any technique as a form of treatment for physical, emotional, or medical
problems without the advice of a physician, either directly or indirectly. The
intent of the author is only to offer information of a general nature to help
you in your quest for emotional and spiritual well-being. In the event you use
any of the information in this book for yourself, which is your constitutional
right, the author and the publisher assume no responsibility for your actions.

Printed in the United States of America.

Also by Peter Francis Dziuban

Consciousness Is All – Now Life Is Completely New

The New, True Infinity

So Be It – How The Nature Of Being Answers
Some Of Life's Biggest Questions

http://PeterDziuban.com

Table of Contents

Why This Book?

Welcome to an adventure in the power of noticing.

Noticing is familiar to all because it is so natural and easy to do. It is as easy as noticing the words on this page.

Inside, you'll go far beyond visual noticing (such as seeing these words) to experience many other types of noticing.

What exactly is meant by noticing? The dictionary says that to notice means to observe or pay attention to.

Noticing is like being aware—but there's a slight difference. Noticing actually is what occurs *thanks to* being aware or conscious.

Imagine a sun-like light so brilliant it can illuminate anything. The light itself, which is always on, is like awareness, consciousness. The *focusing* of the light on something is similar to noticing. It's usually a focusing of attention.

For example, you are aware as these words are being read. It is thanks to first being aware that you are able to do anything. And at this moment, being aware is what enables you to notice and focus on these words.

In the bright light of noticing, many things about oneself, one's world, and the astounding nature of Life itself become crystal clear.

Awareness and noticing are such an integral part of living, that to speak of them in terms of benefit almost sounds silly. It's like saying breathing is a benefit.

Noticing is one of the most natural, normal things that go on all day. It is so effortless, most of the time it isn't even noticed that noticing is happening!

Yet look at how powerful it is.

Noticing basically drives *everything* you appear to do.

Would it have been possible to get the body out of bed this morning without having first noticed you were awake?

Could any meals have been eaten today without having first noticed the food?

Could you have gotten this book without having first noticed that it said something of interest to you?

When noticing is used *intelligently* it becomes priceless.

It can remove whatever might be in the way of experiencing greater happiness, love and freedom.

Chapter Three shows how awareness is a bit like the clear glass of a car windshield. It is through this windshield of awareness that you appear to experience your entire world.

In its natural, normal state, awareness is inherently pure and clear. But it gets covered sometimes with the mental sludge of old conditioning, negative thoughts and emotions, or maybe just *too many* thoughts and emotions.

Then we try to navigate through daily life with all of that stuff obstructing the view.

Noticing acts as wipers which keep the windshield clean and clear.

Another huge benefit of noticing is that it frees you from false beliefs. Beliefs often limit how you see yourself and your world—thereby severely restricting your life. Yet this isn't even realized.

Suppose you were given a hot new sports car. But when it was given, you were put under a belief, like a hypnotic spell: "Use this car whenever you want, with one rule. You must drive it only on your driveway—nowhere else."

One day you snap out of the hypnosis. You see the driveway story was a belief, not a fact—and you are free to go wherever you wish.

Beliefs are nothing but mistaken assumptions parading as facts. They are like mental clouds. But clouds never block the sun from being the sun.

Similarly, beliefs cannot block or limit you once they are exposed. When false beliefs fall away, the limitations and unhappiness they caused fall away with them.

Other times, noticing is just plain fun, and yes, exciting! The wonderful thing is, noticing is much more than a belief remover. It shows how magnificent Life is, in ways previously unimaginable.

Simply Notice follows this author's first work, *Consciousness Is All – Now Life Is Completely New* (Blue Dolphin 2007). *Consciousness Is All* is an experiential book on the nature of Life and Reality for experienced readers of spiritual literature. For reader comments, please visit www.ConsciousnessIsAll.com or for reviews see www.Amazon.com.

Simply Notice says many of the same things, but in a simple, fresh and entertaining way, intended to interest a wider range of readers.

If you have peeked at the pages after Chapter One, you have seen each page stands alone, as a simple noticing of *something*.

The noticing may be about what you consider yourself to be. Or it may be about thoughts and emotions (this is belief territory).

There also is noticing about everyday things, such as bananas and cell phones—or more serious subjects such as the world, and Life itself. Increasingly, you'll see the *value* of noticing, and how various aspects of noticing work.

With each simple noticing comes a fresh seeing, a sharper awareness and discernment. This ends unnecessary struggling and leaves one free to enjoy Life as it naturally, effortlessly is.

So don't think of these pages as a task, as a new project you must take on in order to improve yourself.

This is meant to be a delightful—and at times eye-opening—discovery of how magnificent and free *you already are*.

The noticing on page 15 says: "*Noticing is self-expanding. The more you notice, the more you **notice** that you are noticing.*"

It's really true. So this *Book 1* is first in a series, all with the main title, *Simply Notice*. Each will have its own theme, but thanks to its self-expanding nature, the noticing will spread in many directions.

As you continue reading you may begin to feel, as the author does, that this book could say so much more. That's correct—and it's actually a good thing.

What will happen is that a noticing here will trigger something you will notice on your own. And that will lead to still more noticing.

You likely will ask, "Why isn't the book talking about *this*—and why doesn't it mention *that*, too?"

Countless things *could* be said about noticing.

That's just an indication of its unlimited power.

Introduction

As just mentioned in the Preface about noticing, its very power led to something huge that influenced the writing of this book.

It is, as they say, a game changer.

It may be *the* game changer.

This doesn't mean you continue the same game, and change its outcome. It means suddenly you've got a brand new *kind* of game.

The new game is an incredibly significant fact about the limitless nature of Life and awareness, consciousness.

Bottom line is, there truly is only one *universal* consciousness. It is the very consciousness you are now aware of being—and it is not stuck inside the head of the body holding this book.

Consciousness embraces the entire universe.

These pages enable you to *experience* this, rather than merely reading theories *about* it.

Amazingly, this has been known for centuries. Yet it has gone largely unnoticed by most of us, and continues that way today.

The reason this is not more widely known is because it is hidden by an illusion. That illusion is the way the human senses—mostly sight and touch—make the everyday world appear.

If all this sounds far-fetched, don't worry. Making it crystal clear is what this book is for, and simple steps of noticing walk you carefully through it all.

It's like being invited backstage after a magician's show. You see firsthand how the tricks and illusions work. Exposing the illusion begins in Chapter Twelve, "Yes, We Have No Bananas."

All these points kept coming up during the writing, as if asking for special emphasis—so they became the theme of this *Book 1*. A first glimpse is just ahead in the overview in Chapter One.

You are about to go way beyond "thinking outside the box."

That has long been a popular phrase. Notice something about it now, which you may not have noticed before.

Of course, "the box" means the limits of an old way of thinking.

So you get outside of that box by using a new way of thinking.

But notice that even when outside of the old limited thinking, you're still *thinking*.

So now you've got a new box—but it's still a box!

Thinking is a very useful thing, but know this: thinking *is* the box.

This is an adventure in getting altogether *outside of thinking*.

You are going straight to pure consciousness, unlimited awareness—that which gives rise to, and *notices* all thinking.

This is similar to having a big Aha!

To have an Aha! is great—but notice something about those, too.

The Aha! itself is not really where it's at.

What you want is *where all the Aha!'s come from*.

That's the juice.

That's unlimited awareness.

1 Overview—This Book In One Chapter

To say "simply notice" is a call to attention.

Rather than telling you to blindly accept and *believe* something, it's like saying, "See for yourself."

It sounds funny, but there is a lot about noticing you may not have noticed.

What usually gets the most attention is the *thing* that is noticed or *what* is noticed.

What is noticed can take many forms. It could be an item such as this book or a vivid red tulip. It could be the smell of fresh paint. A change in a tone of voice can be noticed. When you change your *mind* you notice that, too. It is even possible to notice a certain mental or energetic atmosphere when entering a room.

In another sense, it's also possible to notice an *absence* of something. Suppose these words were flowing along, and suddenly a blank space appeared right here   in this sentence. It's like noticing there's nothing to notice.

Then there is the act of noticing, itself. If noticing is like a focusing of attention, who or what is doing the focusing? If awareness is what notices, what exactly is awareness?

Why are some things actively noticed, such as enjoying a sunset, while others are passively noticed, such as the sound of thunder intruding upon the silence?

Then there are many things that seem to have gone unnoticed. Perhaps some of those will soon be brought to light.

Your entire experience can change in an instant when some things that have gone unnoticed are suddenly noticed.

The words *simply notice* as used here are an invitation, too.

They invite you to an entirely new way of experiencing Life, and seeing that Life really is magnificent beyond your wildest dreams. Yes, *really.*

This doesn't mean pumping you up with a lot of inspirational talk.

These pages point out a very different, yet specific and definite way to see or perceive your world, and see what *you* really are.

It is totally natural—and, in fact, it is already happening right now.

It has just gone unnoticed by most of us.

Start with a few things about yourself that may have gone unnoticed until now.

At this moment, there is a "you" that is conscious and aware and noticing these words.

To say, "There is a 'you' that is aware," means to begin knowing yourself more as *a state of awareness*—instead of as just a body.

This "awareness-you" seems able to be aware of other things, too.

The area near your body can be noticed. Perhaps there is a chair on which the body is now seated. Notice it.

Be aware of the feeling of the body's weight against the seat. Really notice the feel. Is it hard or soft?

This you that is aware might be able to notice other things. If there is a window nearby, the outdoors might be noticed; maybe the sky.

Now come back and notice the body again as it is holding this book.

Pause after each of these sentences to *closely* notice the body.

Notice your right foot. Raise it up and move it around a bit.

Specifically, be aware of how it appears—the color and shape. Feel the weight.

Next, slowly pull your left thumb up close.

Really notice the fingernail. There it is—just a fingernail.

Now notice something usually overlooked, yet extremely telling.

That fingernail never notices you.

Always, *you* are the one that notices or is aware of the fingernail.

It never is the other way around.

Stop and see if it ever happens that the fingernail is aware of you.

That fingernail never has said to you, "You've been aware of me all day! Now we'll switch and it's my turn to be aware of you."

Stop and confirm this now with other parts of the body. A whole finger. A leg. Chest. Try a tooth. An ear. Even your entire head.

The answer always is: *no part of the body* ever is aware.

The body never is the same as the you that is *aware of* the body.

If no part of the body is aware—and yet *you* are aware—then you must be something more than the body.

The body is what you seem to *use*. It is not what you *are*.

Awareness is what *you* really are.

Perhaps you never noticed this before. That's okay. Notice it now.

Now take it even further.

Stop again to really notice the body as it is breathing.

The gentle up-and-down rhythm of the lungs is noticed as supposedly occurring *inside* the body.

Go slowly and let these sink in. Notice that the heartbeat, a muscle cramp, and even the taste of toothpaste, are other things that would be noticed as being *inside* the body.

Now notice this book. It appears to be *outside* the body.

Notice other items again where the body is seated. Notice a window if you can. Suppose the moon could be seen through the window.

The book, window, and moon all appear to be *outside* the body.

So—some things are noticed as being inside the body.

Some are noticed as being outside the body.

Either way, inside or outside—*all these things are noticed*.

That's what counts. *Both* the inside and outside things are *within your noticing*. They all have that in common.

It means the muscle cramp and the moon really are found in the exact same "place."

Everything always appears to be going on *within* this state of noticing or awareness.

Be alert that some things appear to be outside the *body*, of course. But nothing you experience is ever outside of noticing or awareness. Otherwise, that thing could not be noticed.

Even the body itself appears to be included within awareness. Awareness is all-inclusive of every last bit of your experience.

The more you notice about this, the more it is clear.

This all-inclusive "bubble" of noticing or awareness really is where the entirety of your universe appears to be experienced.

4

The popular belief today is that you are a body—and awareness, consciousness, is limited to functioning only *inside* that body.

But you've already begun showing yourself the opposite view.

It can equally be said that you are a state of awareness, and this awareness appears to have a body—and everything else!—within it.

The following example is far from perfect, but here's another quick way to get a sense of the difference.

For a moment, think of one of those clear glass decorative balls that have a miniature snow scene inside them.

If you've never seen one, these glass balls are about the size of a baseball. Inside the glass might be some tiny trees, maybe a house, a sleigh, and a tiny person or two. The glass ball also is filled with water and tiny white flakes.

Pick the glass ball up, shake it, and it starts snowing inside.

You are taught to believe you are limited to being like one of the tiny people in the scene. Supposedly, consciousness or awareness is stuck *inside* that tiny body.

What you will see in these pages is that awareness is like the glass.

The glass (awareness) is not inside the tiny people. It includes or embraces everything in the scene.

In other words, the "seeing" is no longer happening as if looking out from *inside* the body. Now the seeing is done from a state of all-embracing awareness.

The difference simply lies in changing what your starting point is—from body to awareness. It's a change of what you consider yourself to be; what you identify *as*.

Don't be surprised if this stirs up some questions, because you've begun to challenge a huge, long accepted belief.

If any of this seems unusual or intimidating, just know that a lot more simple examples of noticing are coming up. All these points will be made crystal clear—that's what the entire book is for—and this chapter is just a quick overview.

On the other hand, if this isn't new to you, please be patient and open to the possibility that you may see something new here, too.

If all things—body, earth, even the moon and universe—can be said to be within noticing and awareness, it changes *everything*.

You need an entirely new way of seeing how Life works.

In the new view, it's as if the perspective is turned inside-out.

Formerly it seemed you were aware or seeing from inside the body.

Now, as awareness, you're not stuck inside there.

All experience, and even what had seemed to be a separate planet earth "out there" with Life on it, now is seen to be *within* this all-embracing awareness, consciousness.

This awareness is not some far off ethereal state that must be attained. It is *this* very awareness you are presently aware of being.

It just has gone unnoticed.

The irony is that none of this is new.

The notion of an all-embracing universal consciousness or Life has been known to sages, saints, and philosophers for centuries.

It gives new meaning to the spiritual saying, "The kingdom of God is *within you*."

Today this is increasingly accepted by scientists. Their way of putting it is to say that there is no world "out there" that is separate from the observer (awareness) that observes it.

Rather than merely telling you this as if it were an abstract idea, these pages allow you to see and live this experientially.

This little scenario may help put its significance in perspective.

Imagine being able to leave this current year, and talk with those who appeared on earth in the year 1000.

One of the first things you might say is, "Hey! Earth is not the center of the universe, and earth is not flat! That's an illusion. Don't let that false belief limit you! There is a new way of seeing things. Earth is round, floating in a vast space."

Now suppose you fast-forward to the year 3000. You are able to look from there, and have a talk with yourself here, today.

You'd likely tell yourself, "Hey, you are not *in* the world. The world appears *in you*. But you aren't what you now believe you are—not a mere body. You are Life's boundless state of consciousness which includes *everything*—even the whole universe—in its alive embrace. The universe really is made of Love, not space."

The 3000-you then says, "Do you realize what else this means? Life is not *on* earth! If anything, earth is *in* Life. That old belief needs to be dropped, like the old flat earth! There's an entirely new way of seeing."

"Earth has gone from flat to round to now being like an idea or concept in awareness! It's so magnificent it becomes indescribable!"

Finally the 3000-you says, "This is true now! It doesn't have to be waited for, any more than the round earth had to be waited for."

This book is the rest of that conversation with yourself.

It is the very Life you are, showing yourself the magnificence of the Life you are.

* * * * *

2 Notice Some Things About Noticing

To simply notice is easy.

On a clear day, how easy is it to notice the blue sky?

The noticing is so easy, so simple, it happens before there's time to think about it.

Simple noticing is the actual *live experiencing* that the sky is blue.

It is not a thought *about* the sky such as, "*Why* is the sky blue?"

It is a direct perceiving that is immediate.

* * * * *

Here's one more example.

Simply notice this page.

Instantly, the page is seen—directly observed.

Done.

The noticing of it was effortless, and a complete success.

What counts is the simplicity.

There is no complicated thinking process about the page—no need to analyze, nothing to *understand*.

Yes, it's possible to think endlessly about this page or the blue sky.

In fact, you likely will *want* to think deeply about much of what is noticed in this book. This is encouraged and often leads to exciting insights.

But that comes after each initial simple noticing, which is immediate.

To enjoy the power of simple noticing, it's not necessary to have an advanced college degree, or to have reached some so-called enlightened state.

The fact that the words in this sentence are now being noticed means you've got all it takes.

* * * * *

Please don't rush to judgment if it seems the early noticing in this chapter might be *too* simple.

Simplicity encourages clarity—seeing Life as it plainly is.

In this apparent age of information, we have become driven largely by *thinking.*

There is nothing wrong with thinking, but it often comes in too fast.

Thinking can obscure or taint natural, pure seeing in Life.

Before something can clearly be seen or perceived for what it is, thinking is already adding judgments and commentary, acting like a smoke screen.

Thinking is coloring the view with a bias toward how that thinking has been conditioned—by family, society, education.

The great mistake and source of so much unhappiness is that this thinking is often based on a set of totally false beliefs.

Yet the falsity isn't even realized!

Simple noticing cuts off, or pre-empts that tainting process.

It enables a direct, live experiencing—a clean, clear perceiving. It is totally natural and wonderfully effortless.

Then thinking can be used *later* to ponder what has been noticed.

This simple noticing naturally feels good—the way it feels good when the garden is clean and not full of uninvited weeds.

Instead of being choked with mental and emotional weeds, Life appears to flourish.

* * * * *

There are many types of noticing.

Besides the visual, noticing can involve sounds, touches, tastes and smells.

It can involve thoughts and emotions.

Noticing can also involve insights and realizations—sometimes called discernment.

It can even include more subtle experiences, such as psychic phenomena.

You'll also be amazed at how much can be noticed about the very act of noticing!

Then there is so much that can be noticed about Life itself.

Noticing makes clear what is essential in Life, and shows what is non-essential and limiting.

All of this has an immediate impact on your experience.

All of this has to do directly with you.

One of the main things that will be noticed is what you really are.

In essence, you really are a state of awareness, consciousness, which is capable of *noticing*. (In this book, awareness and consciousness are treated as synonyms.)

It is this very same awareness present right here, now, that is enabling the noticing of these words.

As this awareness, you are far greater than just the body holding this book.

What will be noticed is that Life itself is what you really are.

* * * * *

While reading these pages, many unusual and new things may be noticed.

That's the whole point.

Ideally there will be plenty of, "Hey, I never noticed that before!"

The noticing of these new things for the first time may lead to sudden insights and even breakthroughs. This, too, is wonderful and encouraged.

Always, what will seem unusual or new is *the thing noticed*.

What is not unusual is the act of simple noticing.

This is always completely natural and effortless—just like noticing that blue sky.

Why devote an entire book to something so simple?

To experience the magnificence of Life is this simple.

Being happy is this simple—if one will only notice.

* * * * *

Noticing is in some ways similar to what is called mindfulness.

But it is not meant here as some type of disciplinary practice.

It is a fascination with Life that happens spontaneously. It goes hand-in-hand with being aware.

The more you notice, it is clear what some key differences are between *noticing* and *awareness*—and these are discussed more in upcoming pages.

Sometimes when doing things, we're very aware and alert, or mindful. It's as if noticing is fully turned on.

Other times, it seems things are done without really noticing.

Things are done almost blindly or automatically, and it's as if noticing and awareness are turned off, or ignored, at least partly.

A big part of this book is devoted to showing that actually, awareness always is "on" in Life.

This awareness is always present and available, and it's effortless.

To enjoy this, simply begin noticing that awareness is already here.

* * * * *

Did you ever notice what happens when *really* noticing something, maybe for the first time?

There seems to be a surge of alertness and vitality.

It's as if there is an upward spike in the awareness level.

Distractions dissolve and you are fully, consciously present.

It might come as a surprise, "Omigosh, that's amazing!"

There might be an exciting realization, "Yes! This is so!"

Sometimes realizations are calm, but with a distinct clarity. Or, they might come with a *feeling*—of freedom, joy, or love.

When there seems to be this jump in awareness level and vitality, it's not really that Life suddenly has become *more* turned on or more present.

Life's vitality and alertness always is *fully* present.

Rather, what happens is that some part of Life that seems to have been ignored is no longer being ignored.

* * * * *

Noticing is self-expanding.

The more you notice, the more you **notice** that you are noticing.

* * * * *

You've probably seen pictures of a baby chick poking its way out of a shell.

At first, some of the noticings in these pages may feel similar.

It may feel as if you are poking holes in some false beliefs that have been confining.

False beliefs are like *mental* shells.

Notice that once out of the shell, the chick never goes back.

* * * * *

If noticing is so simple, why make such a big deal about it?

Noticing shows what you've been missing.

It shows you the difference between what seems to be going on, and what's *really* going on.

It makes clear who or what is running the show in your experience.

You might be surprised to notice how often it's *not* you!

As you'll see, noticing also makes clear there is a definite, specific way Life naturally functions or "works."

No one can change the way Life works.

Yet many of us unwittingly seem to live in ignorance of this, or try to pretend otherwise.

To try to live in a way that is opposed to how Life naturally functions, is to be opposed to the very Life you are!

It makes you your own worst enemy—but it's not even noticed.

Noticing exposes this, and the opposition dissolves.

That is the difference between happiness and unhappiness.

* * * * *

Being aware and noticing is like being awake—instead of asleep and dreaming.

Imagine having a dream.

You probably have noticed one of the main things about a dream.

Virtually always, the "you" in the dream *doesn't realize it's a dream*.

That's the ironic thing about dreaming.

The characters in a dream automatically assume they are wide awake!

The dream characters are not awake.

The dream experiences are not real.

But in the dream, *none of that has been noticed*.

Notice something else about a dream.

As far as the dream characters are concerned, there is nothing *beyond* the dream.

The dream characters have no idea that there is another, *real* kind of awakeness.

A dream character has no idea of what it's missing.

It is the same in daily living when being up and awake—but not really *aware*.

You have no idea of what you're missing.

* * * * *

You might be shocked at how many of today's beliefs are like that dream.

One such belief is that Life is limited to being only *on* earth.

Many today are willing to agree Life may be on other planets.

But notice that they still believe Life is only *on* planets.

This way of seeing or "model" is that Life always must be *on* something.

Generally speaking, this belief of Life being "on" is virtually unquestioned by society.

It is no one's fault because it seems this is all we've been taught.

This book is speaking of an *entirely different* way of seeing things.

It's showing how earth and the entire universe appear to be *in* Life.

The old belief of Life being "on" is like a dream.

To blindly continue to accept it would be the equivalent of the dream characters saying, "There is nothing beyond this dream."

So there is good reason to notice closely and expose some of today's widely accepted false beliefs about Life.

This dissolves the limitations that seem to have resulted from the false beliefs.

Then unnecessary distress and unhappiness automatically dissolve, too.

Unhappiness is caused only by false beliefs about what Life really is.

* * * * *

3 Like A Crystal Clear Windshield

Simple noticing is like being the clear glass of a car windshield.

The clear glass windshield simply provides the view.

The clear glass never *comments* on the view.

When driving down the street, does a clear glass windshield ever say, "I would prefer another scene. Choose somewhere else to drive, please!"?

A clear glass windshield never adds to, or complicates, what comes into its field of view by also *thinking* about the view.

The clear glass doesn't project a judgment or story on the view, and see only *that*.

In other words, things can be seen as they really are.

Simple noticing is the same—it is a pure, raw awareness or perceiving.

Like clear glass, this clear awareness is not cluttered with an overlay of mental chatter due to beliefs or prior conditioning.

Clear awareness is a *silent* seeing.

* * * * *

So—a windshield remains clear, no matter what seems to appear in its view.

Notice how the crystal clear glass always is stress-free, too.

It is the same in everyday living when naturally being aware and perceiving—even right here, now.

After the next line, pause reading a moment.

Keep your eyes open, just relax, and without thinking, be aware *silently.*

This is seeing simply—like clear glass.

There is no internal commentary or judgment *about* what is seen.

This is clean perceiving—as it naturally, normally is in Life.

It is simple and easy.

It literally feels *light,* too, because there is none of the added-on mental weight of thoughts, judgments or feelings.

In other words, there are no added burdens, no stress.

It was said earlier that there are certain ways in which Life naturally works.

This clear, unburdened seeing or awareness is one of them.

This is the Life and awareness you naturally, normally are.

* * * * *

What counts is that this simple, clear awareness or seeing is naturally present *first* in Life.

It functions automatically. It is virtually effortless.

Does it take any effort to simply be aware of this page prior to *thinking* about it?

Notice that there seems to be effort only if thoughts and commentary start up: "What was said back on page 17 again?" or, "I wonder where this is leading."

Only when there are a lot of thoughts or feelings *added on top of* Life's clear direct seeing—only then does Life seem to go from simple to complex.

Pause again—and *feel* what it is to simply, silently "be a clear windshield."

Notice how mentally uncluttered, how open and free this feels.

Enjoy how natural and easy this is.

Now notice if any thoughts come in and try to add their commentary.

If they do, be clear glass with those thoughts, too.

Simply notice them without additional commentary on the commentary!

During the day, pause frequently to be like clear glass.

Notice that the presence of this clear awareness is not something that "you" personally are causing to be present.

It is Life itself that is effortlessly doing all of it.

Feel again how un-tense and unburdened this is.

* * * * *

The clear glass of a windshield need not *struggle* to be clear.

It is inherently clear and need not make effort to be clear.

Clarity is simply its nature.

In fact, it can't *avoid* being clear.

Sometimes rain and dirt may get on the surface of the glass. But underneath, the glass itself remains pure and clear.

The beauty of Life's simple awareness is that it, too, is inherently clear.

All clutter and stress seem to be found on the surface, on the level of thinking and emotions.

These seem to come from personal experiences and conditioning.

All of that, for good or for bad, is what makes up the conditioned personality.

Before thoughts and emotions come in, Life's seeing is clear and *unconditioned*.

Notice that it's as if the personality's activity is *superimposed* on pure, raw Life.

Thinking and emotions are what a personality does.

Being purely alive and aware is what Life itself does.

Feel this easy, natural, clear presence of awareness again—this time knowing it is not necessary to struggle to make it be present.

* * * * *

You may notice a tendency to get caught up in the constant movement of thoughts.

If so, it may seem hard at first to experience this natural calm, clear stillness of raw Life.

That's okay—there's a lot more coming up about this.

Don't fight with the thoughts or try to stop anything.

Rather, just keep noticing and feeling how Life's clear awareness always is effortlessly present underneath all the surface movement of thinking.

Notice how this clear, silent awareness remains perfectly present whether thinking thinks or not.

Notice how, no matter what thinking thinks—Life's clear awareness can't be made to go away!

Notice that Life's clear awareness *simply never is absent.*

This is the real You—and You already are here—so You don't have to *get* here.

Just don't identify with the thoughts that try to superimpose themselves on Life's simple clarity.

* * * * *

What is said here about clear seeing doesn't mean one should try *not* to think.

Thinking and judgments obviously are essential for decision making in daily living.

Fantastic new insights also often come directly from thinking deeply about something.

But when thinking runs out of control—that's what leads to problems and creates its own artificial unhappiness.

It isn't that thoughts and feelings *know about* a state of unhappiness.

The burden of those superimposed thoughts and feelings themselves would be all there is *to* unhappiness.

Meanwhile, Life's clear awareness is always unburdened and immediately present.

It's the way the clarity of the windshield is always immediately present as the glass.

* * * * *

This is not a perfect example, but for now just notice this:

A clear glass windshield can take virtually anything into its field of view.

The one thing the clear glass never can see is *itself.*

A clear windshield never can stand outside itself and see itself as some kind of noticeable thing or object.

The clear glass by itself never could prove it is even there as glass!

But this doesn't mean the glass isn't there.

* * * * *

Notice a similarity to how a clear glass windshield never can see itself.

You never have seen yourself.

To say you never have seen yourself doesn't mean you've never seen your *body.*

Obviously the body has been seen countless times.

By this is meant, you never have seen the noticing or awareness that right now is *aware of* the body.

You never have seen the "you" that is a state of pure awareness or consciousness.

You never have seen that which notices or is aware of thoughts and emotions.

This is the "you" that is Life itself, and not see-able in that way—just as the clear glass windshield can't see itself.

For now, just notice this.

Awareness, consciousness, and perceiving as used here do *not* mean the brain.

The brain, supposedly, is an organ of the body.

Being aware and perceiving is not an organ—it is an experience, an activity, a functioning.

* * * * *

While reading, the thought may come, "All this noticing is fine, but how do I *use* or apply it? What am I supposed to *do* with it?"

It's not necessary to do anything, other than to continue noticing.

When bright sunlight evaporates a fog, leaving only clear seeing—it's not because the sun is trying to apply itself to the fog.

The sun is just being what it is, the sun.

Similarly, just by being the simple, clear awareness you naturally, normally are, the fog of excessive thinking evaporates, too.

This book doesn't say Life will be magnificent only after something is *done* with what is noticed.

It says Life *is* magnificent.

Yes, there is a lot of noticing in these pages.

But each step is a simple one, which effortlessly leads to another.

Soon, the light of Life's clear awareness and natural happiness is unavoidable, inescapable.

It is seen to be the very Life you are right now—not after years of study.

Contrary to popular belief, Life's happiness never is something separate that must be attained.

It is what is right here, *already.*

* * * * *

4 Life Is Not A Hoarder

Notice what typically happens throughout each day.

Most noticing is concerned with *things*, not Life's clear awareness.

Over the course of a day, countless things get noticed.

Imagine trying to count how many items seem to be noticed just visually or by the sense of sight in a day. You could count thousands before lunch.

It begins at home, the instant the body wakes up, with many things noticed in the bedroom.

And that's before seeing what's in the kitchen, the bathroom, the living room, or noticing family members or anything else.

Things are noticed visually about the car, or what is on the street.

There are all the things noticed visually at the workplace.

Many items are seen or noticed multiple times—co-workers, phone, computer, and so on.

If that's not enough—there is everything noticed by way of *sound.*

Voices, birds chirping, dog barking, water running, phone ringing, TV, radio, wind, car engine, on and on.

Even the thoughts in your head are usually experienced as a sound— the sound of "your thinking-voice."

And how many of *those* occur each day?

There is an easier way to get a handle on all this.

* * * * *

First, notice that almost all things in daily living are experienced by way of the five senses.

If some thing is noticed or experienced, chances are it has been seen, touched, heard, tasted or smelled.

As just said, on waking in the morning, the body is often the first thing noticed, thanks to the sense of sight. It is noticed as being in another thing, the bed.

Notice how the *sense of touch* seems to support this.

The tactile feeling of bed sheets on the skin, a feeling of a mattress and pillow—all these touches seem to confirm the sense of the body being in bed.

The *sense of hearing* contributes, too. Perhaps it was the sound of an alarm clock, or voices, which led to the waking up.

Thanks to the *sense of smell*, all this might be followed by noticing an aroma of fresh coffee or toast—and later accompanied by the *sense of taste*.

And so it seems to continue throughout the day.

The day seems to be a constant flow of sensory experience— countless sights, touches, sounds, smells and tastes—some more noticeable than others.

The five senses will be talked about a lot more.

For now simply notice that the senses often involve the experiencing of what are called objects, or tangible items—such as a body, bed, or cup of coffee.

* * * * *

What are other types of things that get noticed?

What about thoughts?

First, consider the extent to which it is possible to notice thoughts.

If you're not certain of your capacity to notice thoughts, think of a banana.

There it is—a yellowish, sort of oblong image in thought.

Now think of a zebra.

Of course, it's easy to tell the difference between that thought of a zebra and a banana—because each is a different image that is *noticed*.

Often, instead of being an image, a thought is just words.

As said earlier, the words usually are experienced as a sound, "a voice in your head," instead of as an image.

Seeing those images and hearing those voice-sounds is all there is to noticing thoughts.

* * * * *

Each and every thought can be noticed—although thoughts can seem to flit in and out so quickly, it's hard to keep up.

Right now, stop and notice one or two thoughts that come up.

Perhaps there's a thought, "This is getting mildly interesting."

Or maybe it's a thought that all this noticing is opening some kind of Pandora's box, and there is a feeling, "I don't want to go there."

That's okay. Notice that, too.

For this little exercise, there is no right or wrong type of thought.

Right now, stop a few moments to simply notice *any* thoughts that come up—even if it's the thought, "I'm not noticing any thoughts."

Is there a temptation to rush on to the next page *for more information?*

Or is there an actual *stopping* to be aware and really notice some thoughts?

* * * * *

Notice if a thought comes up and then there is a *judgment* about that thought.

It might be, "That is a ridiculous thought."

Or, "That is a brilliant insight."

Or it might be the judgment, "There are way too many thoughts going on!"

It might be followed by, "Uh-oh. I shouldn't judge so much."

Sometimes there are even judgments about the judgments!

Simply notice this also.

Even a judgment is *just another thought*—that's all.

* * * * *

You also may have noticed that thoughts often seem to be followed by emotions or feelings.

Perhaps a loved one has been away, and the thought of her/his return leads to a warm feeling of affection.

Or perhaps the thought of an uncomfortable meeting with the boss tomorrow leads to an emotion of dread or fear.

Usually such emotions then lead to still *more thoughts*.

They are like links in a chain of events.

One thought or emotion seems linked to another thought or emotion, and then another—leading you along throughout the day.

What if this chain of *thought-emotion-thought-emotion* were dominating your experience each day?

You'd be kind of *chained*, wouldn't you?

Being chained is not the way to be happy.

What if there were an alternative—but you hadn't *noticed* it?

Life itself is not chained.

Again, in the following examples, there are no right or wrong types of thoughts or feelings, and no judgment.

There is only whatever comes up, and simply *noticing that*.

Be a clear windshield again.

* * * * *

Impartially notice a few thoughts or feelings that come up.

After that, notice something else.

When was the last time a thought or feeling noticed *you?*

Has it ever happened?

* * * * *

Seriously—can you recall the last time a thought or feeling noticed you—rather than you noticing it?

No—because it never happens.

Pause and let this in.

Say you are looking forward to dinner at a favorite restaurant. You've thought of the restaurant half a dozen times during the afternoon.

Can that thought of the restaurant ever change places with you and say, "You've already thought of me six times today. That's your limit—no more!"

On the other hand, could that thought ever say, "I'm going to make you think of me 100 more times today."?

No thought or feeling has its own inherent life, power or intelligence to do anything on its own.

No thought ever can dominate that which perceives the thought.

Notice what it feels like to realize this.

Notice that it feels *free*.

Each time there is simple noticing of this, it's like breaking a link in the chain.

No longer can the chain bind and control your experience the way it used to.

* * * * *

Thoughts *by themselves* have no power to notice or do anything.

Stop right now and really see how impossible it is.

Think of the letter A. See it as an image in thought, in "your mind's eye."

Can that A by itself *ever* notice that which is now perceiving A?

Can that letter A by itself ever change places and say, "Okay, you're done noticing me. Now I'm going to notice you."?

Does that A have any life, intelligence or power to do anything on its own?

Notice that A simply appears to be there. It never acts on its own.

Thoughts by themselves can't *do* anything.

They just seem to come and go.

If you never noticed this about thoughts before, it's not your fault—so don't feel foolish or guilty.

Simply notice it now.

* * * * *

Notice that this is not saying to *stop* thoughts or feelings altogether.

It is saying to simply notice them.

This is what stops the unconscious identification with or *as* them.

This breaks the chain.

It doesn't mean becoming cold and insensitive, or a mindless robot.

Rather, you *use* thoughts and emotions instead of them using you.

Thoughts and feelings are merely what seem to come and go.

They are merely what you seem to *have*.

They are not what you *are*.

* * * * *

Thoughts can be likened to billboards on the highway that pass by.

Thoughts are like *mental* billboards that pass by.

When riding in a bus on a highway, suppose some billboards appear to go by.

Could any billboard ever change from being a mere billboard?

Or, could any billboard suddenly leave the roadside, get on the bus, take control and start driving?

Sounds silly, doesn't it?

The thing is, thoughts sometimes can be more subtle than billboards.

They may seem to come and go almost under the radar—until they are *noticed.*

How often are rushing, random thoughts allowed to drive the bus in daily life—without really being noticed?

Yet why should a bunch of mere flitting, mind-less thoughts be the controlling force in daily affairs?

It sounds foolish—especially since no thought can notice or do anything by itself!

Is any thought by itself intelligent or aware?

Or is it a mere unaware thought?

* * * * *

If this noticing of thoughts seems new, it may lead to even more, new kinds of thoughts.

Notice any thoughts or feelings such as, "Now that I see this, it's so obvious. I should have known this before."

Don't latch onto them because they would be just more links in a new chain—and they lead right back to being bound.

Most importantly, notice that *no thought* has any inherent power of its own to control or influence you or your happiness.

Invariably, thoughts and feelings will arise, yes—but one need not always accept or act on them.

Do you act on what's said on every single billboard you pass on the highway?

If you did, you'd never get anywhere.

You'd be stopping at every motel, gas station and fast food restaurant along the way!

They're just thoughts.

* * * * *

If it ever seems as if thoughts are bombarding, sit back and calmly notice.

They might be thoughts and feelings of pressure or inadequacy.

They might be pushing really hard: "Get to my next appointment... Get the kids to practice...Get groceries during practice."

Instead of being pushed around, pretend you're at a dinner party.

See this serving of thoughts as if they were hors d'oeuvres on a tray.

They are being offered up to you.

It might seem tempting to accept them, to grab hold of one or more.

After all, they are constantly in your face.

Simply notice that it is possible to say, "No thank you."

Notice how free, how unchained this feels.

* * * * *

If thoughts can seem like mental billboards, notice that emotions can seem like undercurrents.

Emotions, too, can seem to quickly take over and pull you right along with them in daily living, just like thoughts.

Emotions as meant here, refer to feelings such as fear and confidence, depression and elation, frustration or satisfaction, resentment or sympathy, etc.

Each emotion usually has its flip-side, or opposite.

Sometimes emotions seem more subtle—like invisible currents of electricity.

What counts is that emotions are *felt*.

They aren't something that can be seen like a billboard—which is why emotions sometimes are not noticed as readily.

If your body ever goes swimming in the ocean and there is an undercurrent, it definitely is felt, although it may not be visible.

Just because something is not *visible* doesn't mean it's not *noticeable*.

The difference between emotions using you—or you using emotions—is the extent to which they are noticed.

This is easy once the noticing is on a *feeling* level, instead of a thinking level.

Then if emotions seem to suddenly pop up, they can be noticed for what they are and dealt with appropriately—rather than them controlling the day.

They can be treated like hors d'oeuvres, too.

* * * * *

So—thoughts can be like billboards and emotions can be like undercurrents.

Now what about Life's pure, aware seeing or noticing?

What is Life's pure perceiving—*distinct from thoughts or emotions that seem to be perceived*?

It's like asking, what is a clear glass windshield all by itself—distinct from what appears in the view?

The simple, clear presence of Life's awareness never is a billboard.

Life's clear presence never is an undercurrent or feeling of pressure.

It simply is present.

Thoughts seem to move, come and go.

Emotions, too, always move, come and go.

Whatever appears in the view of the clear glass comes and goes, too. But the clear glass never alters.

Life's capacity to simply be aware and perceive never alters either. It doesn't come and go. It is always calmly, effortlessly present.

It may seem at times as if Life's calm, clear presence is overlooked or covered over, but actually it *never* is absent.

Feel again how delightfully effortless and light Life's clear, aware presence is.

Feel again how *unfailingly* it is present.

* * * * *

Sometimes in daily experience, situations seem to arise without anyone being able to control events.

Notice that what can be controlled is the *response* to the situation.

One need not react blindly like a link in a chain of events.

Suppose the phone rings while eating dinner with the family.

It's an aggressive telemarketer. You politely tell the caller you're busy and want to hang up.

The caller gets more aggressive, then rude and angry. There may be a temptation to get angry and react accordingly—a chain link.

Suppose just prior to calling, the telemarketer was told by his boss, "If you don't close a dozen sales tonight, you're fired."

Notice the links of the chain.

Notice there was no anger before the phone rang.

One feeling or thought during the phone exchange leads to another, escalating into an ugly situation.

WIthout *noticing* all this, these feelings and thoughts play out their story—and you are entirely manipulated by the links in its chain.

Blindly reacting makes one a mere puppet of the story.

By noticing, one is free of the chain and can respond calmly—resulting in an entirely different experience.

* * * * *

Did you ever notice how skilled actors can quickly change their emotional life during a scene?

A versatile actor is able to express the full range of emotions.

To do that, emotions must be allowed to come and go.

The actor is free because there is no bondage to any single emotion.

There is neither resistance to them, nor any clinging to them.

Good actors are like Teflon. Nothing sticks.

On a scale of 1 to 10, all emotions rate a 5.

The actor fulfills the role to the very best of his/her ability, but always knows it is all make-believe.

Throughout the day, play your role to the full.

See how many 5's you can notice.

Then notice what it feels like to be Teflon.

* * * * *

Just like a clear glass windshield, Life's clear awareness does not hoard or *accumulate* views.

Whatever appeared in the view of the clear glass yesterday has come and gone. It isn't present today because nothing sticks.

Life, as it naturally is alive and aware is just like that—a pure, *present* seeing.

It is not an old thought.

It is not an old emotion.

Life's clear awareness always stays, or *is*, in the present tense only.

Notice that this *present-only* nature of Life simply is how Life is naturally being alive and functioning, right here, now.

This, too, is how Life "works" and cannot be changed—so why let thinking try to oppose it?

Again, Life's clear awareness *does not think*.

Only *thinking* seems to think.

Life's pure awareness is not a hoarder of everything mental and emotional—beliefs, resentments, regrets or desires.

Notice if thoughts and emotions come with a temptation to cling.

Notice it's possible to say, "No thanks. Life is not a dumpster."

Life's awareness is naturally fresh and clean, not cluttered, and this can't be changed.

So there's no point in trying to pretend otherwise.

* * * * *

When reading, are you an underliner or a highlighter? Perhaps you like to mark passages that have significance.

If so, you've probably noticed when going back later that the passages sometimes don't have the same impact. Or, new ones jump out that weren't underlined before.

(This author knows—he used to be a world champion underliner!)

Notice something about this whole process.

Life's ease of clear awareness stays perfectly present if something is underlined or not. It is not dependent on underlining in a book.

Relax and silently be a clear windshield for a moment. Notice again that Life's clear-seeing presence *never* goes away.

Really feel this *un-go-away-able-ness.*

Now notice closely what it would feel like if *nothing* were underlined. At first it might feel like letting go of a security blanket.

Now notice what's *behind* that feeling.

There might be a feeling of nothing to hold onto. There is only a kind of openness; maybe it feels like a free-fall, or a freedom.

But notice that Life's awareness still is *perfectly* present!

This open freedom is Life itself being present—the real You!

Life *doesn't need* anything to hold onto!

Yet Life never fails to be perfectly present.

Can you stay free, and not underline—even what's on this page?

Dare ya.

* * * * *

5 Notice Whose Life This Really Is

Nothing is more basic to living than Life itself.

Have you ever noticed some essential things about Life itself?

Life itself as used here is meant universally, in the broad sense—in terms of all the Life there is.

Life itself is not referring to any one, single body. It does not mean the sum total of any one person's individual experiences.

It means the one Life which is the Life of *all*.

However, to say "Life itself" equally is not referring to a Life far off somewhere.

It is *this* very Life—that which is alive and aware right here.

* * * * *

Now notice something that may have been taken for granted.

The functioning of Life—*this alive presence of Life right here, now*, is not something that you personally are doing or making happen.

No person, no body, knows how to make Life now be alive or operate.

No body personally causes or sustains Life itself all day long by keeping a foot on the gas pedal of Life's aliveness.

Only Life itself knows how to be alive, to be Life.

Life itself is doing all of it.

This simply is one more way in which Life functions.

It can't be changed.

Stop reading a moment to really notice that not you, nor any other body, personally is causing Life to now be alive and be present.

Yet here Life is, being vitally alive.

* * * * *

This is why the word *Life* is capitalized.

It shows that the presence and functioning of Life itself actually is impersonal.

In the greater sense, this Life that now is being alive here, really is Life's life.

It really is not "your life" because, again, the functioning of Life is not something being done by a personal "you."

The fact that Life is impersonal doesn't take anything away.

Life, your body, and everything else is still right here.

If anything is taken away, it would be the misconceptions and stress arising from a mistaken belief that Life itself is a personal ability or responsibility.

This also means that *right here*, there is always something functioning that is far greater than "little me" and all my personal concerns.

* * * * *

There is a vast difference between *Life itself* and personal experiences in *daily living*.

At times, the experiences of daily living may seem difficult.

For Life itself to simply be alive is always easy.

A big point of this book is that this *ease* of Life itself is what you really are.

For some, it may appear as if experiences of daily living have been challenging and unhappy up until now.

There is even an expression: "I'd really like to turn my life around."

It literally is possible to do that very thing right now.

Turn it around.

In other words, instead of starting out as one little personal life and seeing everything in terms of it, turn the perspective around.

Look out from, or begin to "see" in terms of the one Life that is *all* Life—rather than a single body that appears to be *in* Life.

See in terms of the whole, not one little part.

After all, it really is the job of Life itself to be alive and aware here, now—not "you."

Much more will be said about this—but this simple yet fundamental switch in perspective is one of the most important steps of all.

* * * * *

Life itself is not just an abstract intellectual concept.

Life is an actual *alive* presence, a presently *living* experience.

Life is the *alive feeling* or presence that is actively being vital and consciously aware right here, now.

To experience this *aliveness* of Life may seem new or a bit unusual.

If so, calmly take inventory of what is going on with you right now.

According to the sense of sight, there appears to be a body holding a book.

Other things can be noticed by the sense of sight—perhaps furniture and a room. Stop reading to notice them.

There may be other sensations, such as the feel of air temperature where the body is sitting. Notice that feel.

Then carefully notice any sounds. Notice the sound and feeling of breathing. Take a moment to let all these "register."

Now stop reading to notice some thoughts as they arise. Think of a green apple. Now think of a white cat.

Watch how the thoughts *come* and *go*.

One moment a thought is there, then it's gone.

Soon, a new thought comes up.

Notice also that there is *something* which is noticing or perceiving those thoughts.

But that which is noticing is not the *same* as those thoughts.

* * * * *

Now tune in on an even finer level. Close your eyes if you wish.

As any thoughts arise and then leave, try to notice what is present *in between* the arising of thoughts.

What exactly is left after a thought has gone?

Momentarily there is a kind of opening. It is as if there is an open space in which this thought activity seems to come and go.

Really try to notice the nature of this open space in between thoughts. It may feel calm—a kind of quiet, free feeling.

It may feel like nothing—even boring.

Notice that it is not possible to *think* what this open space is.

The moment that's attempted, you've got a thought—and not the open space.

Notice how this space or open feeling in which thoughts seem to arise is not the same as an object or a form.

This space is not like a green apple, or a white cat—it is not a *thing*.

It is *no thing*.

This open space has no form, no appearance. It is invisible.

But it is not a total deadness either.

If you tune in closely, whatever this invisible open space is, you can feel it is gently *alive*.

Even though it may be *no thing*, it definitely is *present and alive* as no thing.

If this seems new, be sure to allow yourself time to feel, or *be alive as* this alive open space. Otherwise, it will seem abstract, just an idea—and not the *consciously alive experience* it actually is.

* * * * *

This open, alive space could be called Life's *aliveness*, or *presence*.

Sometimes this alive presence or open space is called pure awareness or consciousness.

Notice if there are any thoughts trying to say this open space or alive presence is abstract, or sort of woo-woo.

It *should* seem that way to thinking because to thinking this *is* abstract. But it seems abstract or woo-woo only to thinking, not to Life's aliveness.

Put it this way: is it woo-woo to be alive, aware? Of course not.

Recall about thinking outside the box—and then getting even outside of thinking. That is what this open, pure awareness is.

Notice any thinking that tries to object to this. It might, because it means thinking no longer is the only game in town.

Instead of getting stuck on that, treat this alive, open space like an unexplored new realm.

Notice this alive presence is not a *belief,* and not this author's theory—because beliefs and theories consist of thoughts.

This alive, aware presence is not being *thought.* It is purely *alive.*

Having no form or appearance, this alive open space of Life's pure awareness is not the same as the *content* that appears to be *in* awareness, such as green apples or white cats.

Notice again that only *thinking* seems to think and have beliefs.

Life's awareness doesn't believe because awareness does not think.

It only is purely *aware.*

A clear glass windshield simply is clear—it does not *believe.*

* * * * *

The calm, still aliveness of Life's presence may seem faint at first.

It may seem a bit elusive, almost like a soft whisper.

To Life itself, its own aliveness actually is full, clear, vital—never faint or obscure.

What seems to obscure this calm is a tendency to notice only the obvious things—sights, sounds, touches, thoughts and feelings.

That's the most obvious activity, so it gets most of the attention.

It's like having a TV playing loudly in the room, and not being able to hear someone across the room whispering to you.

The whisper is definitely *there*, potentially perceptible, but it seems covered over.

So notice if there is any attitude or judgment about the value of this invisible calm, this alive open space.

Thoughts may try to come in and belittle it as a waste of time.

Life's aliveness is quiet, gentle—but this doesn't mean it isn't *powerful*. You'll see it is truly all the presence and power there is.

Without struggling, continue to simply notice and tune in to how effortlessly and unfailingly Life's open presence is alive and present.

* * * * *

Now stop to closely notice and feel how this open, gentle aliveness *never is absent*.

See if it is possible to notice this gentle aliveness *not* being present.

It is like an invisible, yet alive *ever-present-ness*, or presence.

It may seem covered over at times, but it always is present where you are because it *is* the very Life you are.

Relax and just try to feel, or be alive as, this calm, unfailing present-ness of Life's aliveness.

Specifically feel how *easy* it is for Life's open aliveness to be present and alive.

It isn't really that a "you" is turning attention *to* this aliveness.

This aliveness literally *is* the very presence of Life itself—because only Life itself can be this aliveness.

This is the real You because only *this* is what is actually being alive and aware right here.

Much more will be noticed about Life's aliveness.

For now, simply notice that it never goes away.

* * * * *

As you have seen, the noticing is now on a finer "feeling" or presence level, rather than on a visible, tangible or thinking level.

Just because this calm presence or open aliveness seems to be on a finer level—that doesn't mean it is less valid or real.

Perhaps it has just gone unnoticed until now.

Notice also that the words in these pages didn't *put* Life's calm, clear aliveness here.

The words have just pointed it out.

It is *always* here.

* * * * *

Notice if there is any feeling of, "How will all this make me better, a more successful *person*? How will all this improve *my life*?"

It is natural to want to be happy and harmonious, but the key is to have the right "Life."

The way to appear to have a better personal experience is by not starting on the level of the person.

The way to best apply this in daily living is to not try to apply it, but to simply *live it.*

The only way Life really "works" is that all living is Life's living.

Life itself is already fully satisfied and harmonious.

The key is to start here—which is why all of these noticings are about Life itself.

This doesn't mean one's personal affairs will be lost sight of or ignored. Rather, it is as if they become injected with Life itself!

But to start out with a personal self exclusively is to start with a self that is cut off from Life itself—and always is subject to problems, limitations and part-time happiness.

Have you ever noticed Life itself not successfully being Life itself?

Does a clear glass windshield ever fail to show up, and be one hundred percent perfectly present—regardless of what is in view?

* * * * *

You're at a wine tasting party.

At the tasting party, that is what it's really all about—tasting.

There may be discussion, too, because with wine, there is plenty that could be talked about.

Countless books have been written about wine.

It seems there is no end to how much can be *learned about* wine.

Yet if all those books were piled together, and all their learned ideas discussed—it wouldn't begin to approach the *taste* of a single sip of wine.

The two simply cannot be compared.

* * * * *

This book is for *tasting* what Life is, not learning more information *about* Life.

This is why all the emphasis on simply noticing, rather than thinking.

This is not for learning facts *about* Life, as if Life were something conceptual or separate.

This is for tasting Life's *aliveness* as living, functioning presence right here, now.

It is not intellectual.

Life's easy, light *aliveness* is what much of the noticing here is devoted to.

The point is to constantly "sip" and "feel" or *be alive as* the very Life you are.

What is learned or known may be wonderful—but it is always conceptual, once removed, and not actual *Life.*

Again, Life in its essence is *alive.*

Life's aliveness is only *live*-able, not think-able.

Taste, *be alive as,* this exquisite, unfailing ease of aliveness.

Take big gulps repeatedly.

It's very intoxicating—and there's never a hangover.

* * * * *

Notice what all of this indicates about the very *noticing* going on right now.

It really is Life itself that is being alive here in the first place—in order that all noticing or perceiving can occur.

So all of this really is being done thanks to the presence of Life itself—not thanks to a personal "me."

Then who or what is it that really is interested in noticing and perceiving—evidenced by the very reading of this book?

Is it really "your" interest, personally?

It may seem that way, but actually, it is thanks to Life itself.

Pause to notice this as you read.

It changes everything.

* * * * *

6 Life Turned Inside Out

Imagine a jigsaw puzzle, with all its pieces mixed up, sitting on top of a table.

Now imagine being one of those puzzle pieces.

There you are—only a tiny fraction of an inch high, right on the level of all the other pieces.

As a puzzle piece, it's impossible to see the big picture.

When not down on the level of the puzzle, seeing the big picture is far easier.

To see or be aware as if looking from inside one little body, is to be seeing as a puzzle piece.

To see as Life's awareness, is to not be on the level of the puzzle.

From here, putting together the pieces of day-to-day living and seeing how Life works, is from an entirely new perspective.

* * * * *

Everything noticed or perceived on an everyday basis is usually put into one of two categories—whether it is realized or not.

As touched on in Chapter One, things are perceived as being either *inside* the body or *outside* the body.

A few quick examples again, just to be clear:

Breathing. Feeling of fullness after a meal. Toothache. Emotion of happiness.

These would be said to be experienced *inside* the body.

Blue sky. Car. Tree. Ocean.

All of these would be said to be experienced *outside* the body.

There are cross-over situations, too.

You're eating a slice of pizza.

One moment it appears to be an object external to the body. Then it turns into a few bites and some chews.

Suddenly it's fully internalized as a great taste, and a warm satisfying feeling inside the stomach.

From the so-called normal human perspective, that's basically it.

Things are experienced as inside the body, outside, and some can be both.

* * * * *

Why does it seem everything is noticed as either inside or outside the body?

In other words, why are things always noticed *in relation to the body*?

Why is it *that* way?

It's because the body is where the noticing or perceiving is assumed to be occurring—it is said to be occurring *inside* the body.

Suppose the average person on the street were asked, "How does noticing take place in your experience?"

They would answer, "Noticing happens because *I* do the noticing."

Almost always, this "I" that notices is said to be the body, and is said to be *inside* the body.

Notice that when seeing from a *body's* perspective, some things, like the blue sky, seem to be "out there."

They only seem to be "out there" due to first having *assumed* there is an awareness or perceiver located "in here" inside the body.

You may be interested to know that with all its incredible findings, science never has been able to find awareness, consciousness, anywhere inside the body.

* * * * *

Look again at what happens regardless of whether some thing is noticed as being inside the body or outside the body.

Either way, it is *noticed*.

Either way, it is something one appears to be *aware of*.

In other words, the overall capacity to be aware takes in *all the things.* All the things inside the body *and* all the things outside the body appear to be *within* awareness.

Seen in this new way, the blue sky is in the exact same "place" as breathing—both appear to be within awareness, perceiving.

Even the body itself appears to be in awareness.

So in this new way of seeing, there no longer are *both* inside and outside.

This isn't a perfect way of putting it, but in one sense all experience now might be called "inside"—meaning it all appears to be *within* noticing or awareness.

Awareness is the one, all-inclusive place in which all experiencing of Life is found.

It's never otherwise.

* * * * *

Consider the moon, sun, the stars and even the endless universe a moment.

All of these, too, appear to be *way* outside of the body.

Yet, in another sense, the only "place" all of them are found—ever—is as part of, or within, all of that which is being noticed or perceived by awareness.

Pause reading and really let this in.

Needless to say, the stars appear to be way, way beyond or outside of the body.

But is it possible to find stars outside of, or apart from, the awareness of them?

Of course not, because if they were outside of or beyond awareness, they couldn't even be noticed or be said to exist!

So while some things might appear to be beyond earth, and way outside of the body—*never* could anything be beyond or outside of awareness.

* * * * *

Even *imaginary* things are within awareness, perceiving.

What are called out-of-body and near-death experiences also occur as part of awareness or perceiving.

Otherwise, how could they be described by those who have them?

What is it to stop and realize that *no thing whatsoever* can be said to exist outside of the awareness or perceiving of it?

Life's awareness is unlimited and all-inclusive of all there is.

This is not referring to an unlimited awareness that is abstract, or in some distant, esoteric state.

It is true of *this* awareness which is perceiving right here, now!

As this state of awareness, what does it feel like to not have limits?

* * * * *

What if, for just a moment, it is *not* first assumed that the perceiving is occurring from inside the body?

What about when seeing from, or as, Life's all-embracing awareness?

In this way, it is as if everything from the body to the universe—is "right here" (in awareness) and there is no "out there."

It is called *Life's* awareness because, again, this perceiving awareness is not something that "you" personally are doing or causing to function.

It may seem "you" personally can choose to think, talk, have feelings, and do other things.

The fact that awareness is now functioning is thanks to Life itself. It is not the doing or choice of a person.

It will become increasingly clear that because awareness is all-inclusive of all there is, it means awareness literally could be called Life itself.

Life and awareness are just two different words for what is the same, *one*, all-embracing presence which is simultaneously alive and aware.

The word labels Life and awareness are like Joseph and Joe—just two words for the same one.

* * * * *

Look slowly around the entire area where the body is now seated.

Really do this.

Notice the floor—slowly—its color, and where it meets the walls.

Take time to notice all the walls.

Now thoroughly notice the ceiling.

The ceiling appears to be beyond, or outside of the *body*, of course.

But the ceiling and walls are not outside of this all-inclusive state of noticing or awareness are they?

Just as the book and body are things included within awareness— notice the ceiling, floor and walls all appear within awareness, too.

Then what's the next question?

Where are *you* as this awareness?

As this awareness, you can't be *inside* the room. Why?

Because the entire room appears to be within you.

It is the *body* that appears to be in the room. Awareness cannot be found or located inside the room.

You are not now confined inside a room or body as this book is being read.

* * * * *

Noticing a blue sky is no different from noticing a ceiling of a room.

For the blue sky to be *included* within Life's awareness is no more difficult than including a ceiling of a room.

The sky obviously seems to extend much farther beyond the body than a ceiling does.

But the sky never is outside of, or beyond, awareness, perceiving.

Put it this way: where *else* would the sky ever appear to be?

As Life's awareness, you are not *under* a sky.

If anything, a sky appears to be "under," or within, the aware Life you are.

What does it feel like to be greater than even the sky?

* * * * *

Suppose the body were outdoors and there is a clear blue sky.

Now strip this experience of all hearsay and assumptions.

Get it down to raw experience.

All that's *actually happening* is an awareness of what appears as a blue color. It's just a visual image. There also might be an image of a body and some surroundings—more colors.

For this raw experience, nowhere inherent in it is there anything to prove that, "I, the one aware of all this, am here, *inside* the body. And the sky is *out there*, apart from *me* here, inside the body."

There is nothing to indicate that is actually the case.

All that is present is a state of awareness which appears to include a blue color called sky, a body, and other items.

Nothing is being designated as either inside or outside.

That would be just a subtle presumption or assumption.

A presumption is basically a *pre-assumption*. It's something that is *pre*-assumed to be true, prior to an experience.

The thought, "I am aware inside the body as this blue sky is experienced," is *presumed*.

Who is saying such a thing? The sky isn't saying it. The ground isn't. Not even the body is saying it. Only *thinking* presumes it because that's what the thinking always has been told.

Thinking may seem to be inside the body, but not awareness. And *both* thinking and the body are found only in awareness.

Actually, Life's raw awareness itself never *says* anything, not even "everything is within awareness."

Life's awareness simply is aware. Keep it raw.

* * * * *

Life's awareness does not have to strain or do anything special to include the sky.

Is it ever possible to notice Life's pure awareness making any struggle?

Be alert that if there seems to be any struggle, it would be *thinking* that is struggling, not awareness.

Awareness is effortless in its capacity to include everything—even the sky and universe.

Again, how does this effortlessness feel, as alive stuff?

* * * * *

Suppose it were possible to somehow meet right now with what some might call God, the Divine, or "The Ultimate."

Whatever that term may mean to you—how would it be known for certain that this God or Ultimate had been met?

Wouldn't this God also be part of, or *within*, all of that which is noticed or perceived?

If not, how else could it be noticed that God had been met?

Stop reading and really look until it's clear.

Without the awareness or perceiving of this God—it would not be possible to say this God even were there.

So which would be greater—this God, or the perceiving *which includes even God*?

Some might say, "Well, any kind of noticed or perceived God wouldn't be real. It would be merely a figment of imagination, just a mental image or concept."

It is often said God can't be directly perceived because God is the Infinite.

The Infinite cannot be reduced to something noticeable or perceptible.

Okay, but even that very realization—to notice that God, the Infinite itself, *would not be noticeable*—is a very important kind of noticing.

In other words, it has been noticed that perhaps there are some things that can't be noticed—at least not by way of normal noticing!

* * * * *

73

Watch closely what goes on when reading some of these noticings.

First there will be the noticing. Say it's the one on the previous page about God.

Then there may be a *reaction* to what has been noticed.

Notice that reaction very closely.

The initial simple noticing and the reaction to it are very different things.

For example, the reaction may be one of confusion, or a vague sense of, "I don't get it."

Or, the reaction really may be one of, "I don't want to let that in."

If so, try to notice these closely, too.

It's one thing to honestly not understand or not be clear about what has been said.

It's entirely different to not want to *accept* it.

When long-held false beliefs are exposed, much of the time we clearly "get it."

But there can be a reluctance to *admit* it.

Notice if this happens.

* * * * *

When noticing has exposed a false belief, there can be a feeling of having done something wrong—due to having accepted that belief.

It can make you feel foolish—as if you fell for a silly superstition.

There is no reason to feel foolish because these are not *your* beliefs.

They seem to be beliefs generally accepted by humanity, and they often are all we're taught.

Many times we're not given an alternative.

This is no one's fault—so there is no shame in it.

Notice that letting go of old beliefs can be treated another way.

It's like sensibly letting go of the baggage when you're at your destination.

There's no need to carry it anymore.

* * * * *

A transition is gradually occurring in these pages—to one of seeing from above the level of the puzzle.

That is what all these early noticings do—literally change the "level" from which the perceiving seems to be happening.

It clarifies things which, beforehand, might have been inconceivable.

Society and education usually teach you to see in only one way. It is as if the seeing is from within a physical body, contained inside a very limited thing.

This body-self seems to be only one among many other such body-selves—all of them supposedly separate from each other.

Now the perspective is shifting—from inside to out—to seeing from, or as, Life itself, the one all-inclusive Self.

Now the seeing is not contained in any one thing.

Rather, the seeing appears to embrace all things.

It may not yet be clear where all this is going.

Seeing from the same level as the body, the five senses, and thinking—is seeing from the realm of illusion and belief.

When not on their level, it is much easier to then look down upon them and see how they seem to operate.

This is what exposes their illusory nature.

* * * * *

7 Mission Impossible: Find "I"

Suppose you were asked, "Are you aware right now?"

The instant response would be, "Yes, of course, I am aware."

But what, exactly, have you said?

Who is this *I* that is now aware, conscious? See this *I* in what is perhaps a new way.

Say the word "I" to yourself *silently.*

Do not voice I aloud. Let I be said only silently within.

Say "I" very slowly and very softly. Let this I keep repeating itself— very slowly and easily—"I," "I," "I."

Keep going slowly until you clearly hear this I within yourself.

Then try to closely notice the nature of that which is saying I.

What is important is that which is doing the saying. The *word* I being said is not so important.

What can be noticed about the nature of this voice that says "I"?

This I-voice is not the same as some thing that can be seen, such as a book or a body, which is *visible.*

Notice that "I" is like an inner voice that is *invisible.*

In doing this, do not first identify yourself as the visible body and assume it is the one now saying I.

Start or identify directly as this *invisible* I-voice only. Deal only in terms of invisible I, all by itself alone.

* * * * *

The saying of "I" is not taking place by way of a physical mouth or vocal chords, is it?

It is clear that "I" is being said—but I is not being heard by way of physical ears, is it?

Can the fingers touch I? No. Nor can I be tasted or smelled.

I has nothing to do with the five senses.

Notice that when saying "I," the visible body never changes places and becomes this invisible I.

In the same way, invisible I never becomes visible as the body.

This *I* that is voicing itself is invisible-ness *only.*

Invisible I by itself is not like a physical object with a form. Rather, I is form-less.

You cannot find any hard, physical edges or border to I, the way physical objects like this book seem to have.

I has no physical length, width or height as its dimensions.

I is *un-dimensional.*

I, in terms of itself alone, has no solidity like a body; no thickness or density. If anything, I seems to be an incredible *softness.*

Meanwhile, this voice, this I-ness, seems to be a specific, distinct *presence.*

This I that is voiced is like an *invisible presence* rather than a *visible person.*

So when saying "I am aware," one cannot be referring to the body, because the body is not the I that is aware.

* * * * *

Now take it further.

Notice when "I" is *not* voiced.

First there is the voice "I." Then there is nothing, silence.

This silence *in between* each inner voicing of I is the quiet inner space mentioned in Chapter Five—it is a silent, open stillness.

But it definitely is not *deadness* because you still are alive, aware, even though "I" is not voiced.

Notice that, like the I-voice, this still, alive silence is invisible, too. It is not even something that can be thought or conceptualized.

Now notice that when the invisible I is voiced inwardly, it seems to be kind of ethereal.

Somehow it is clear "I" is being voiced, yet invisible I can seem elusive. It is hard to hold onto, or pin down.

Notice also how the I-voice seems to come and go. It's temporary.

When voiced, the word "I" seems to arise out of pure awareness.

Then the I-voice seems to leave, dissolving back into the stillness.

Now notice that the moment "I" seems to arise as a voice or thought, it is already starting to fade out or leave.

The I-voice is like a phantom.

Pause again to notice the difference between the arising of the I-voice and the absence of I—the calm, gently alive, open stillness.

* * * * *

If one were to ask, "What is *I* 'made of'?" this I-voice seems similar to having a *thought*.

Thoughts are also sort of ethereal, elusive, and hard to hold onto.

Yet it is clear they are being thought.

Like the I-voice, thoughts, too, often come and go as an invisible inner voice.

And like the I-voice, thoughts seem to arise out of the stillness.

Notice the similar nature between the voice "I" and other thoughts when the "inner-you voice" is normally thinking.

They seem to be of the same stuff.

Now notice something very significant. Without the specific inner voicing or thought of I, *there is no I.*

I not only ceases to arise.

I literally ceases to exist.

It's not as if there is an "I" hanging around somewhere, *waiting* until it is voiced again. That would be just an assumption.

Unless there is the specific voicing or thought, no I can be found anywhere. I has no permanent life or presence of its own.

Life's awareness is present, *you* are present, and the body still appears to be present—but there is no I.

Notice again what is present without the voicing of I. There is only the naturally open, clean, *alive* silence.

Life, awareness, is present, but "I" is not.

* * * * *

Rather than trying to "hold onto" the alive, open stillness, notice something else.

Actually, this aware stillness *can't and won't go away.*

It never leaves—because it is Life itself. Only this is what is alive and aware here, now.

This is the real You.

The "I" comes and goes. Again, it is merely transitory, temporary.

Notice that when I is voiced, there is an awareness *of* the I-voice, but which is not the *same* as the I-voice.

Even the I-voice is just something that Life's awareness, the real You, seems to temporarily be *aware of.*

The I-voice *can't* be You because even when "I" is absent, *You are present.*

Life's open, alive awareness is *always* present, *always* alive.

You do not personally cause it to be present. Only Life does that.

Life itself really is the only one alive here so that "I" can be said—and yet Life does not need to voice "I" to perfectly be the Life it is.

Feel how Life's alive openness never shuts off from its aliveness.

Feel how Life never is blocked from its own aliveness.

Is there a limited supply of Life's open aliveness—is it a matter of physical volume, such as only a few liters?

Or is Life's silent aliveness like an endlessly supplied fountain of gently alive peace—which never runs dry?

What is it to be alive as this *never-runs-out-ness?*

* * * * *

What does it mean that "I" seems to arise only periodically—and that it's impossible to find an "I" as a *permanently present entity?*

This "I" is often called the limited or finite, *personal* sense of "I."

Many books have been written about this "I" by everyone from spiritual teachers to doctors.

Generally speaking, the "I" is said to be the personality, ego, or personal mind.

It is the so-called localized mind or self, assumed to reside in each specific body or person.

In a deeper sense, that which *notices* the "I" is often said to be the greater, unlimited presence of Life's awareness itself.

Life itself, the real You, is invisible, infinite—having no form or location.

As Life's awareness, You are always present "pre-" the voicing of I, and whether I is voiced or not.

In some spiritual teachings and religions, this is known as the I AM, the Divine I or Divine Self.

It is not any one body or person, thus is not personal.

It is present and functions impersonally, infinitely.

* * * * *

Notice that this page appears to have a visible rectangular shape.

It has visible, measurable borders or *limits*, where the page appears to begin, or come to an end.

The body holding this book also has visible borders or limits where it appears to begin and end.

What about the I-voice? Although not visible, it still is noticeable, too, as something awareness seems to be *aware of*. It also is limited—having a beginning and end—one moment it's there, then it's not.

Notice that, *always*, all beginnings and endings, all borders, all limits, are found in the things or forms one seems to be *aware of*.

Now what about Life's pure awareness—distinct from the I-voice and everything else you seem to be aware of?

Can the awareness that perceives this page be said to have borders or limits—like a rectangular page or a body?

Stop and see if you can find such a border. Is it possible to find a wall—even a mental wall—where invisible alive awareness *stops* being alive and comes to a clearly defined end?

That which is *aware*, that which appears to perceive this page, has no limits, no discernible beginning or end point.

How can you know this for certain? Suppose you said you *did* find an end or limit to awareness. How would that be known?

That very end *also* would have to be something you were *aware of* in order to say it was there.

So—even this so-called "end" would be something *within* awareness.

Thus awareness really wouldn't be ended or bound by it at all.

* * * * *

As Life's awareness, aliveness, has no noticeable form or limits, it cannot be said to have any measurement.

Where would a ruler be placed on *invisible* awareness in order to begin measuring?

Then Life's awareness, aliveness, really cannot even be said to be like a windshield, or round like a glass ball.

Those are imperfect examples, used only to make certain points.

A big flaw of the windshield example is that it implies a seeing is taking place from *inside*—inside a car. Be alert that the use of the windshield example is not meant to imply Life's awareness is similarly inside the body.

As Life's measureless awareness, you are presently alive and aware— yet totally formless and limitless.

Since Life's awareness has no edge or end-point, how could it be confined *inside* a head or brain?

Stop to consider it. If awareness were confined, it would have a border and come to an end where the head or brain ends.

Awareness has no such border or end.

What does it feel like to be vitally alive—yet have no length, width or height?

If all this seems abstract or of little value, notice it is speaking of *You as You really are*—not a mere limited visible body.

* * * * *

This inability to pin down Life's awareness or give it a form may seem frustrating at first.

The thing to notice is that it seems frustrating only to the thinking mind, not to awareness!

Notice that any frustration merely would be something that is noticed, too!

It actually makes perfect sense that the formlessness of awareness may seem elusive to the thinking mind.

It's because the thinking mind's very job is to try to give a mental form to, or conceptually grasp things.

Yet there is nothing about pure awareness itself to be grasped.

So—it is becoming increasingly difficult for thinking to get some of what is being said here—*and this is how it's supposed to be.*

This is important to notice—and nothing to be alarmed at.

Life's awareness *is not trying* to mentally grasp or pin itself down.

It simply is being aware, period.

Be open to the possibility that this un-grasp-able-ness may be good news.

The fact that awareness cannot be physically located or mentally grasped simply indicates how *unlimited* awareness, aliveness, is.

This shows the unlimited-ness of that which is perceiving all this here, right now.

* * * * *

What is it to notice that, because Life's awareness, aliveness, is *invisible*—it cannot be said to have any color?

Do you realize what this means?

As Life's invisible aliveness, *You* have no color.

You cannot honestly be said to belong to any one race.

How could *invisibility* belong to a race?

Invisible awareness, pure aliveness—which appears to notice all bodies—is not the same as any noticed body of any noticed color.

As the invisible aliveness which is now noticing all this, *You* do not belong to a mortal race—and never have.

If anything, all races appear to be embraced equally by the one Life's impersonal aliveness.

* * * * *

Notice any thoughts or feelings that come up in response to all this.

There may be a feeling of, "I'm not sure I want to be invisible or unlimited."

Or, thinking may say, "I don't deserve to embrace *all there is*. I don't want all that responsibility."

Notice again that Life's capacity to be alive and aware here, now, is not a *personal* ability.

Nor is it a personal *responsibility*.

This simply is another way in which Life "works" or functions.

Life *cannot fail* to function and be present this way.

The capacity of Life's awareness to be unlimited and embrace all there is, is infallible.

It takes no work or responsibility on the part of a person.

Nor can any person claim personal credit for this.

Since this cannot be changed, why let thinking or old beliefs try to pretend otherwise?

You are not merely some insignificant *thing* that is *in* a universe.

As Life's unlimited awareness, the entire universe effortlessly appears to be *within you.*

Have you ever sat back and actually enjoyed this fact?

* * * * *

Notice that it really is not accurate to assume a "you" has risen to a higher state of awareness or perceiving.

It may *seem* that way, yes.

But it really isn't that an "old you" has gained some awareness, some clarity.

All awareness and clarity "belong" to Life itself, and Life is *always* present in full.

What's happening is that some old superimposed thinking and clouds of belief of an "old you" are fading away, or evaporating.

What remains is clear, fully aware Life.

When the blue sky appears to be clear after a storm, it isn't that the clouds have taken on some blue-ness.

The clouds have evaporated.

All that's left is the blue sky which always was present.

* * * * *

8 The Blue Sky Never Struggles To Be Blue

When something is simple, how do you know?

Most of the time, it's because it's easy and it *feels* easy.

But what exactly is being felt when something feels simple or easy?

Maybe it's better to ask what is *not* being felt.

There is no feeling of struggle, no feeling of tension.

It sounds funny, but when something is simple, it almost feels as if there is not much to feel.

It is as if you are alive and fully present, but there is no burden, no work that has to be done.

There is just a feeling of lightness—a wonderful ease.

Sometimes it's almost like a happiness.

Notice this.

* * * * *

Right now, tune in and notice how it feels when something is beautifully *simple*—when something is wonderfully *easy.*

Have you ever noticed a clear blue sky struggling to be blue?

Try to feel how easy *that* is.

Relax into the incredible, delicious *ease* of that.

Feel whatever this feeling of ease and lightness is, even if it feels like "nothing."

The more it feels like nothing, the better.

Notice that you can pause this way and be like the blue sky, be this ease, almost whenever you wish.

And it doesn't cost anything.

* * * * *

When something is easy, did you ever notice that somehow it feels sort of inherently *right* that it be easy?

The ease just naturally feels good.

There even may be a feeling deep down, "Things *always* should be this easy!"

Did you ever stop to question why this is?

When things are easy and simple, it is no accident that it feels natural.

Ease and simplicity are the very nature of Life itself, the Life that is effortlessly all-embracing here, now.

It's just like that blue sky.

Feel again how effortless it is for Life's awareness to simply be present now.

This easiness, this simplicity, literally is what *You are*, as Life's present awareness.

This is why ease feels so natural or inherently "right."

It's what led you to pick up this book.

* * * * *

Consider when something seems difficult.

Say it's the task of fixing a leaky sink.

The area under the sink is crowded with pipes. The wrench is the wrong size, and keeps slipping. Water is running all over.

The leaky sink has plunked itself down in the middle of your day with its whole package of complications and feelings of difficulty.

Contrast those feelings of complication and difficulty with blue-sky *easiness*.

Again, how does easiness *feel*?

In comparison, doesn't easiness or simplicity feel kind of clean or empty?

This ease is like an *absence* of those added-on feelings of frustration and complication.

The feelings are said to have been *added-on* because they weren't there before the sink was leaking.

When living is easy and simple, there is none of the added-on baggage.

The point is, easiness is always what is naturally, normally present first in Life—*as* Life itself.

Ease doesn't have to be created or attained in Life.

Ease *is* Life.

It still may be necessary to fix sinks at times.

It's just a matter of not taking on the baggage while doing it.

* * * * *

The enjoyment this book offers is not gained by racing through these pages.

There is no benefit in trying to reach the end as soon as possible.

The real enjoyment and value come when the reading stops momentarily.

Perhaps it's after having read only a page, or just a sentence.

The enjoyment is a matter of quietly "being with" what is noticed.

There may be an Aha! or two.

Mostly there is a gentle ease and lightness—a kind of happiness.

And what is noticed is seen to be not mere words, not a theory—but a *living* reality.

It feels as if ease, lightness and happiness are all rolled into one— and it is *alive.*

This alive ease is Life "experiencing itself" as Life really is, right here.

* * * * *

Noticing does not mean struggling.

While reading, a lot of new noticing may seem to happen.

That's the whole idea.

However, while reading, also notice if there are any feelings *about* noticing.

There may be feelings of, "I *should* be noticing so much more! I've got to *work* at this until I'm a better noticer."

That is not how noticing is meant here.

Noticing is effortless. It just seems to happen.

So if there is a feeling of pressure, obligation, or a heavy sense of burden to "do" something better—simply notice that feeling, too.

See it as a mere passing feeling—another wanna-be chain link.

Don't claim it as "your" feeling. Don't act on it.

Be alert, yes.

Notice, yes.

Struggle?

No.

* * * * *

Notice this difference in feel right now:

First sit back and just relax.

Don't try to do anything. Not physically. Not even mentally.

Just "bask" in the feeling or natural ease of *simply being present* without wanting a single bit of more information.

Then contrast this ease with the feeling of pushing and tension that wants to rush on to the next page to get more information.

Can you feel that difference?

The ease is natural, normal. The feeling of pushing is something added on.

There is nothing wrong with information.

But don't get pushed around.

Next time the push is felt, simply notice it and say, "No thanks."

Here is one of the most useful pieces of information in this book:

Life's clear seeing and ease—*as it is simply being*—is not dependent on information!

Does a clear blue sky need more information in order to be blue?

* * * * *

Notice one thing these pages are *not* saying.

They are not saying that you *should* live this way, or you *shouldn't* live that way.

They simply are saying to notice how *Life itself* naturally is present and effortlessly functioning.

Life functions the way it functions whether a personality agrees or not.

If a personality wishes to ignore this or tries to oppose Life itself, that's up to the personality.

But that's what leads to personal unhappiness.

Notice it never will change Life itself.

* * * * *

Noticing is its own reward.

With all the noticing going on while reading, be alert if there is a thought, "I can't get a handle on the purpose of all this. Where is all of this leading?"

Noticing and awareness are not supposed to be leading anywhere.

This is about *awareness itself*—and pure awareness or perceiving *itself* is not a "where," not a goal.

One value of perceiving is in staying free from the mistaken assumption that everything always *should* be leading somewhere!

Now turn the perspective around.

See as Life itself.

What if, as all-embracing Life itself, you *already are being* the "ultimate"?

What if, as all-embracing Life, you already are perfect, happy and totally satisfied *forever*?

What if everything that tried to say you were *not* already there was a dream?

It would mean you don't *really* have to get anything or go anywhere—because you're already there.

All that's necessary is to wake up from the dream that you're *not* already there.

* * * * *

Feel, or *be alive as,* Life's gentle, ever-present ease of awareness.

Relax and really feel the *aliveness* of this aware presence.

As this simple aliveness, feel how aliveness never shuts off.

Notice again that the only one alive here, now, to be experiencing Life's aliveness *really is Life itself.*

It never is an experience being had by another.

Notice how Life's aliveness cannot avoid or escape being the aliveness it is.

Life cannot ignore its own *alive-ing.*

This is simply how Life functions—with no effort.

Now notice where your identification usually is.

If the identification is with, or as, *thinking,* it seems as if thinking can flit in and out, and sometimes ignores aliveness.

When the identification is directly *as aliveness,* Life is always already "at" or *being* its aliveness.

So why not be directly alive as aliveness—instead of assuming it requires *thinking* to access it?

Aliveness need not think first in order to be the aliveness it already is being!

Notice again that it is *Life* being this aliveness—this isn't something a "you" has to do or know how to make operate.

The experiencing of aliveness right here truly is the presence of Life itself.

* * * * *

Don't feel it is necessary to remember everything that is said in these pages.

Just stop and notice that Life's awareness does not function on the level of thought or remembering.

Yet the ease of Life's awareness *never fails* to be perfectly present.

Does the clear glass of a windshield need to remember anything in order to be the clear glass it never fails to be?

* * * * *

9 A Movie Screen That Is *Alive*

Usually, noticing is focused on one specific thing.

It is as if attention is directed to a particular item—such as a page of this book right now—to the exclusion of other items.

At this moment, other items across the room are not being given attention.

This focusing seems to be an *intentional* or *directed* type of noticing.

If suddenly there were a loud clap of thunder outdoors, most likely that would be noticed, too.

That noticing would be more unintentional than intentional—but it still would involve a momentary focusing on the sound.

* * * * *

In contrast to the focused nature of noticing, Life's raw awareness or perceiving is of a more all-inclusive or comprehensive nature.

It's similar to a movie screen.

Everything in the movie picture appears on the screen.

But no one thing in the picture is singled out by the screen for focused attention or perception.

After reading this page, stop and lift your gaze away from this book and out across the room (assuming your body is now in a room).

Try not to allow attention to focus too much on any one specific thing.

Relax and let awareness just "take in" the whole room.

There is always an overall awareness that is non-focused.

This awareness appears capable of including or perceiving all things in the room impartially, including the body.

Parts of the room may be temporarily outside the range of the *eyes* while the head is turned a certain direction.

But when the head turns again, none of it is outside of awareness, which is all-embracing.

* * * * *

Try to see in a new way.

Try to see the body, this book, furniture, and anything else—see all of these as if they were appearing in a scene of a movie.

Be aware of this entire scene as if standing back from it—as if all of it were on a movie screen.

The *body* appears to be in the scene—but that's not you. There also is an awareness that appears to be *aware of* the body and the entire scene.

In other words, the body as it now sits holding this book isn't doing the seeing or perceiving of this scene. The body is just another one of the items *being seen*.

This is a new sense of the body—not as the one witnessing the movie scene—but as one of the things *being witnessed*.

It is as if a "screen" of awareness effortlessly includes it all.

This awareness appears to witness not only the body, the room and furniture—but also breathing, thoughts—everything.

Continue to be aware of the body, but don't think of the body, that person, as "me."

Instead, let there be a silent, impartial awareness of the body—as if it were someone you don't know, just a person in a movie scene.

Like a movie screen, there is no *personal* identification with any item.

This is Life's natural, *impersonal* seeing because there is no identification as just one limited person.

What is it to be aware in this impersonal way?

What is it to *continue* being aware in this way?

* * * * *

Continue taking in the room as an all-embracing awareness or alive "screen" instead of focusing on any one item.

If a phone were to suddenly ring, it might seem as if attention becomes focused again as that ring is noticed.

Yet even with that focusing—the room, the body, and all items in it do not suddenly vanish from awareness.

It is as if the all-inclusive "screen" of this alive awareness continues to include everything appearing in the room.

It's similar to all the items in the field of view of a camera lens.

The photographer may single out one item of many in the view and center the picture around it.

But the clear glass lens continues to include the rest of the items that appear in the view.

* * * * *

Keep noticing how the room and its contents appear to be within this screen of awareness—all of them impartially.

Things sort of "automatically" appear this way.

Notice that there is absolutely *no mental struggle* for Life's awareness to be aware in this way!

Stop reading and feel, really relax into, this complete absence of any struggle.

Now notice if any thoughts arise about all this.

Notice how these thoughts would be merely another type of *content* that this awareness seems to include.

Notice that any *emotion* arising would be a type of content, too.

The thoughts and emotions are not visible. They do not appear in the room like the furniture, or the body.

But they still seem to arise within this same awareness.

Notice again how Life's awareness always is *simply present.*

It is making absolutely no effort as it appears to embrace all items.

It is as effortless as the blue sky including a few clouds.

It is not present because of anything being done by a person.

Feel again how this effortless awareness is gently *alive.*

This alive ease simply is another way in which *Life itself* is presently functioning.

* * * * *

Notice what's really happening on a movie screen.

During a movie, the characters appear to move from *here* to *there*.

In terms of the images on the screen, it may even appear as if the characters cover great distances in the movie scenes.

Notice there is another way to see this activity.

From the perspective of the screen, the characters always are *right here*—on, or within, the one screen the entire time.

In the movie, images of a dozen countries may come and go—but none of it ever moves *off* or *outside of* the one screen.

From the perspective of the screen, all places in the movie, even outer space, appear in the same one place.

Always, they are *right here* on the screen.

It's the same for Life's all-embracing awareness as it is alive right here.

Always, there is only "right here"—everything appears within the "screen" of Life's awareness.

* * * * *

Suppose a movie screen itself were *alive, aware.*

It's similar to what was said earlier about the glass ball with the snow scene. It is as if the clear glass were alive.

Try to feel that this all-embracing "screen" of awareness, as it now appears to include the body and room, also feels *alive.*

It's almost as if the air filling the room were alive and aware.

Put it this way: this awareness which embraces all of the room is not dead.

Deadness cannot be *aware.*

* * * * *

Hold up the thumb of the right hand.

Bring it up close to look at it.

Start to really focus on the fingernail.

Notice that if this thumbnail is all that is focused on, this is practically all that will be experienced.

Small as it is, it seems capable of blotting out almost everything else.

Notice how constricted this feels.

Focusing only on the thumbnail is like having a wide-angle lens on a camera, and switching to a super-narrow focus.

Notice which one—narrow focus or wide open—allows the greater variety of experience.

In the same way, focusing exclusively on one body is *really* small, in comparison to embracing an entire universe.

During the day, notice if excessive attention is focused only on "my body" and "my personal affairs."

Is this narrow, personal body-focus acting as a thumbnail in your experience?

It could be blotting out a much richer variety of experience!

Until this is noticed, you have no idea of what you're missing.

* * * * *

Notice that Life's all-embracing awareness actually cannot limit or focus itself.

It cannot thumbnail.

It may seem that *personal thinking* and the *five body-senses* can focus attention on some things to the exclusion of others.

Life's infinite awareness cannot restrict itself or focus on only one thing in that way.

It's like the movie screen not being able to focus on, or limit itself to, only one character or item that appears on it.

Life remains all-embracing, non-focused, regardless of whether personal attention focuses on something or not.

This effortless non-focusing is the real You.

Notice that, *at any time*, Life's calm, all-embracing ease can be presently experienced.

At any time, it is possible to not focus on, or identify as, a body or thoughts.

It is possible to be alive as Life's unlimited awareness, which always is "on."

It need not be activated or turned on.

It is present automatically and effortlessly—and *never is absent*.

* * * * *

During the day, notice if attention goes off frequently with thoughts and emotions.

Notice how these seem to obscure the simple present-ness of Life's effortless clear awareness.

They seem to act as a distraction that temporarily is *superimposed* on pure Life.

The thought or emotion is like a cloud, temporarily appearing in the open blue sky.

But notice that the blue sky doesn't stop being present.

Regardless of whatever thoughts or emotions seem to arise—Life's perceiving *still* is present, still present tense—and it's effortless.

Notice this.

See if it's possible to think something so intense that it makes Life's presently aware perceiving *not* be present.

Does it happen?

Suppose a firecracker were to suddenly go off right next to the body.

Notice that the body, the person, might react.

Yet even if a huge distraction seems to be superimposed on Life's impersonal awareness, it still remains present tense, all-inclusive.

* * * * *

When functioning as Life's impersonal seeing, notice there are no *worries* here.

The body still appears to be present, but not worries.

This shows that it isn't really the *body,* the person, that worries.

Only worrying worries.

Worrying is like a cloud of thoughts and emotions that tries to superimpose itself on pure Life and the body—which are inherently worry-free.

Notice that it's possible to identify not with worries—but to simply rest as Life's clear impersonal seeing.

Worrying is just thoughts and feelings that come and go.

Worries are not pure Life itself. *Worries have no Life of their own.*

For worries to live, they would have to be *enlivened*—they would have to be *given* some of the un-worried pure Life you are.

This is a good occasion to be selfish!

This doesn't mean one won't care, or will be irresponsible in daily living. It just means worrying won't dominate the day.

Does this seem like too easy a way out, or almost like cheating when it comes to dealing with worries? Does it seem as if this is ignoring something?

Notice that it is simply being honest with pure Life as it is alive and perceiving here, now.

And honestly, isn't it *Life itself* that really is being alive here, now, to begin with?

To be honest, Life is worry-free.

* * * * *

10 Notice Like An Astronaut

Notice something about Life's awareness as it is presently being aware and enabling the reading of this.

Being aware is *always in the present tense*.

The awareness that is aware here, now, is not being aware one second ago, or one second from now.

It is aware *now*.

Notice that Life's awareness cannot be aware *other* than now.

Notice that this never changes.

* * * * *

Peter Francis Dziuban ~

You are an astronaut, way out in space.

As the astronaut, you look out of your spacecraft window upon what appears as a small sphere called earth.

At that moment, you know your spouse is home in Houston, Texas. Your son is attending a university in London. And your daughter is on a trip to Hong Kong.

What time is it?

Suppose you judged from the perspective of each of those family members.

Each is in a different city where the local clocks all show different numbers.

On this localized basis there seem to be three different times.

From your astronaut perspective, it is clear that all three cities appear to be in the same one place (earth), all "embraced" at once.

From your perspective, it is *now* for all three cities.

It is not three different times.

Notice that the sense of time depends entirely on perspective.

* * * * *

Suppose, as the astronaut, you look out at earth again twelve hours later according to the clock.

It appears the planet earth has rotated in relation to the sun.

Where it had appeared to be daytime in Houston and night in Hong Kong—now that is reversed.

Yet from the all-embracing astronaut perspective, it is still *now* for all apparent places.

Notice that this *now* applies to all points on earth—not just those three cities.

Notice that *this now does not change* regardless of how earth appears to rotate.

It's like the clear glass of awareness again—always present tense only, or *now.*

Notice that it never is *not* now.

* * * * *

As the astronaut, suppose you were to shift your gaze away from earth, and out across the apparent vastness of the universe.

It is *still* the same now—"everywhere."

It is *now* not only for all points on earth, but throughout the observable universe.

Notice again that this now never leaves, never becomes *not*-now.

Seeing as an astronaut, or from a "universal" perspective, it is *always* now, everywhere.

That's because even the entire universe appears to exist only *within* Life's awareness—and Life's awareness is always *present, now.*

Here's the most important thing to notice:

To take this now-perspective, it is not necessary for the body to be up in a spacecraft.

It is always possible to notice *it is always now, everywhere.*

* * * * *

Notice something about the very noticing of now itself.

How is it possible for you to even be aware that it is now, the present, right *now*?

It is only because Life's awareness is present now, too.

If there were no awareness present now, it would not be possible to be aware of anything—not even that now is *now.*

What's really going on is that the *now* that seems to be noticed, actually is not something separate from this present awareness.

The present-ness of Life's awareness as it includes all there is, literally *is what* now, or the present, is.

The presence of Life's all-embracing awareness here, now, and what is called *now,* are simply two different word-labels for the same thing.

The present isn't something separate from awareness that awareness is *aware of.*

What is called "the present" *is* awareness itself, being present.

See if it's possible to find *another* present, another now—*apart* from this present awareness.

* * * * *

Look at it another way.

Did you ever ask yourself what *makes* now be present now?

Where does this thing called "now" come from anyway?

And why is it *always, always* now as far as you are concerned?

Notice that it is impossible for you to escape the fact that it is always *now.*

Equally, it is impossible for you to escape awareness as it is being present *now.*

That's because now literally is what *You* are, as Life's ever-present awareness.

Now being present is *You* being present, as Life's awareness.

* * * * *

Totally apart from astronauts, notice that right now, it is *now*.

Pretty obvious, right?

The fact that it is now, right *now*, is so obvious, so out in the open, it is usually not even noticed.

One reason why *now* can be overlooked is because now seems elusive.

Now cannot be grasped when one goes to *think* about it.

It's exactly the same as pure *awareness*, which can't be grasped by thinking either.

This *now* that awareness *is*, simply cannot be held onto by thinking.

There's a good reason why.

Now is *now*.

Now is not any time. Now is no-time.

Meanwhile, thinking always takes time. Thinking occurs *in* time. Thinking about what this very sentence says takes time.

Even if thoughts happen super-fast, that's still time.

So the fact that all thinking takes time means thinking *never* experiences now or no-time.

Notice that now simply *cannot* be accessed by way of thinking.

It's not supposed to be.

Yet here now unfailingly is, being now right *now*, as awareness.

* * * * *

Now often is said to be "the present moment" or the present.

Usually, however, this "now" is considered to be a kind of super-brief moment that is experienced in between past and future.

Now is said to be a fleeting instant in the flow of time.

This is how now or the present generally has been understood by humanity.

When it is clear that *now* is the same as Life's ever-present awareness, now is seen in an entirely different light.

Imagine an old-style clock.

The clock face is white with big numbers on it.

Just above the surface of the white face are the clock hands, moving around the face in a circle.

The main thing to notice is that the clock hands never stop moving.

In contrast, the clock face never moves.

This is not a perfect example, but when it comes to *now*, treat now like the white clock face.

The hands of the clock appear to move on the surface, but the clock face itself is not *in* that surface movement.

In the same way, there is no *now* in the movement of time.

Now is not a super-brief instant in time's flow because now is not *in* time's flow.

Now is now—totally outside of time.

* * * * *

To be clear about now, separate it from *thinking* because thinking is time.

Thinking, too, always moves on the surface like clock hands.

Stop to notice that the capacity of awareness to be *present now* is not controlled or influenced by thinking.

Thinking cannot think now *into* being present.

Now is present before thinking thinks, and whether thinking thinks or not.

No amount of thinking can make now *not* be present now, either.

In the same way, no amount of thinking can make Life's pure *awareness* not be present now.

* * * * *

Notice closely that when *now* is used here, it never is referring to "your thinking" *about* now.

This is *not* saying that "your thinking" should try to be as successful at being now as now itself is.

The beauty of *now* is that it is perfectly present without any assistance from thinking!

That's because Life's awareness, too, is perfectly present whether thinking thinks or not.

Does a clear blue sky need any assistance from clouds in order to be the clear blue it already is?

* * * * *

Notice that *now* is not something that can be seen with an eye, heard with ears, or touched with a finger.

Now cannot be noticed as if it were a separate thing, the way a book appears to be sensed.

Now simply cannot be *found*—so don't waste time trying.

Notice that Life's pure awareness equally is not some thing that can be seen with the eye, heard, or touched with a finger.

Again, this is because now and awareness are just two different *words* for what is the same, one ever-presently aware stuff.

As noticed earlier, a clear glass windshield never can see itself.

In the same way, Life's awareness never can see its now-ness—because *now* is not something separate from awareness that could be seen.

* * * * *

Pause reading after the next sentence.

Feel how Life's all-embracing awareness is making *no effort* in being present now.

Really stop to enjoy or "taste" this delightful ease with which awareness is *simply being.*

Equally feel how *now* is making no effort to be now, either.

Speaking of things being easy—for Life's awareness to be present right now, *as now,* is the easiest, simplest thing there is!

In the same way, notice that now never is the least bit *hesitant* in being present.

Nor is Life's *awareness* ever hesitant in being present.

For Life's awareness to be present now, *as now,* is effortless—yet notice how definitely and infallibly present it is.

* * * * *

Often it is said to "live in the now" or "stay in the present."

Instead of struggling to get a better foothold in the now, turn the whole thing around.

See if now can be gotten rid of.

After reading these next couple of sentences, put the book down and try to make now *not* be now.

Try—really try—to make now go away.

Notice if it is possible to ever *escape,* or get away from the now that is now.

Notice how awareness never can escape being present either.

Next, let thinking think very strenuously, and *mentally* try to make now not be now.

Try flailing your arms *physically* to scare now away.

Not even wishing, hoping or praying will influence now to go away.

Notice how this effortless presence of now is un-go-away-able.

After all such attempts to influence or escape *now* fail miserably, notice something else.

You never can escape *yourself* as a state of present awareness either, can you?

Notice that this is all totally natural.

It is simply another way Life functions, or *is.*

Living in the now isn't something you *do.*

Now is what You effortlessly *are,* as ever-present awareness.

* * * * *

Notice again how Life is alive right *now*.

Relax. Close your eyes after the next few sentences.

Then notice, *feel*, Life as it is actually being alive, vital, *only* now.

Be specifically, consciously *alive as* this present aliveness.

This present aliveness cannot actually *be alive* one second ago, in a past.

Life cannot *be alive* one second from now, in a future.

A past or future isn't *alive*.

The only "time" Life is actively alive, vital—is now, in the present.

Life's all-embracing awareness is alive *as the present*.

Notice that this *never* changes.

Now look at it another way.

Could Life *not be present* and still be alive?

Is it possible for *yesterday* to somehow be alive *now*?

See if the very aliveness alive here, now, can stop being *alive now*.

* * * * *

As Life is alive only *now*—then only *now* is alive.

Now is not some dead, abstract idea about timelessness.

Now is *alive stuff.*

Now is the only "place" Life's actual *aliveness* is found.

* * * * *

It really is Life itself that is being alive here, now.

Life being alive is not a personal ability.

Now's capacity to be present now is not a personal ability either.

Notice that another one of the "ways" Life functions is *as this alive present-ness* of *now.*

The now-ness that Life's aliveness is, simply cannot be changed.

So wouldn't it seem foolish to try to oppose Life itself?

Wouldn't it be foolish to pretend it's *not* now, and try to live yesterday, or live tomorrow?

Surely you have noticed it's impossible.

No wonder this is a basic cause of unhappiness.

It would be trying to work against or oppose the un-oppose-able— Life itself, the very Life You are.

This doesn't mean one won't make plans or have goals.

It doesn't mean one won't have memories.

It's just clear that Life always is *now* when these things are happening.

While there still seem to be thoughts in terms of past and future, no longer is there any attempt to *live* in a past or future.

* * * * *

Instead of assuming you are the body that is holding this book—live a new kind of Life.

Act as if *now itself* is what you are.

Be alive as this effortless, all-embracing awareness that is present now.

It's like being the stillness of the pure white movie screen—instead of a character in the moving scenes appearing on the screen.

The difference is that this screen of now-awareness is *alive*.

Feel how this now does not budge from being now.

Now is un-budging.

As now itself, relax, rest, as the un-budging-ness of your now-ness.

It is *alive* un-budging-ness.

It is *effortless* un-budging-ness.

* * * * *

In the same way that now does not budge, stop and feel that Life's *awareness* does not budge.

Hold up an arm and wave it back and forth quickly.

Notice how the arm constantly changes position—over here, then over there.

Yet the awareness which perceives the waving always is unmoving— always *present here, now,* to perceive it.

This un-budging-ness of now is *what* Life's perceiving is.

Feel again how this un-budging-ness is *alive.*

Taste again this *ease* with which Life's awareness is present now, and infallibly so.

Is this ease with which now is present ever *not* easy?

* * * * *

After each of the sentences below, pause reading a few moments.

To quickly read ahead for more *information* is to rob yourself.

Listen how *silently* now goes about being present now.

Is now ever not silent?

Let this silence feel like an *endless expanse* of quiet.

This immeasurable quiet is Life's pure awareness as it is silently being present—the way clear glass is silent.

Feel the delicious ease of this silent now—contrasted with the push, stress and "mental hardness" of thinking and information.

Now feel how *softly* Life's silent awareness is being present now.

Life's silent awareness is not physical; it has no materiality. So it has no hardness or solidity. It is unspeakably "soft."

What is this soft silence as an *alive feeling* here, now?

* * * * *

Feel how exquisitely *gentle* Life's silent awareness is in being present now.

Let this gentleness of Life's *now* feel like a silent sea of Love.

Life's silent sea of Love is *endless.*

It is the sea without a shore.

It effortlessly embraces not only all seas, but an entire universe.

Life's silent Love is *so* boundless that even to say "boundless" feels like a limit.

Notice that, no matter how busy the *body* appears to be during the day, Life's quiet, gentle sea of Love *always* is present.

Notice that Love's silent, gentle *now* never leaves.

It *can't* leave.

Life's gently alive Love literally is *all there is of all that exists.*

There is nowhere besides boundless Life that Life could go to!

This gentle, ever-present ease is Life's natural happiness.

* * * * *

11 Life Beyond Your Wildest Dreams

The focus of noticing will shift for the next several chapters.

It will shift away from Life's ease of present awareness, to noticing more about the five senses.

The reason is that the senses seem to create illusory appearances.

The senses seem to fool us by making the world and daily living appear other than they really are.

Some illusions are minor—such as an illusion of a mirage in the desert—and they have little impact on daily life and society.

Other times, an illusion can have a huge impact.

As said at the beginning of this book, one such illusion appears to be affecting your every waking moment of every day.

Yet this illusion for the most part has gone totally unnoticed by the general public.

Even more important—illusions give rise to false beliefs, and the false beliefs severely restrict how we live.

* * * * *

Before getting into specifics, it helps to put all this illusion talk in perspective.

The biggest breakthroughs in the so-called history of man often involve a dramatic change in ways of seeing, or understanding.

What basically happens is that old, limiting beliefs are seen through, or new discoveries are made.

What these dramatic breakthroughs often boil down to is a simple matter of *noticing* something that wasn't noticed before.

The classic example of breaking through illusions and limiting beliefs would be the now-clichéd flat earth.

The following may seem as if it is badly overstating the obvious. It's done only to refresh your thinking about the power and influence of un-detected illusions.

It's also a warm-up for exposing the other illusion that is largely unnoticed today.

Supposedly, earth at one time was believed by some to be flat and so massive that it was the center of the universe.

It could be said this belief was not accepted by civilizations worldwide—but it helps illustrate an important point.

Of course, the realization eventually came that earth is a relatively tiny sphere, apparently floating in a vast universe of space.

The key question to ask is, "*How* could such a belief have started?"

It was due to two illusions.

* * * * *

Both illusions involve the human sense of sight.

The first illusion is the earth's horizon, which appears flat when seen by a human body standing on earth.

Of course, the body's limited sense of sight is incapable of seeing the earth's natural curvature.

The second illusion involves planetary movement.

Each day (or night), the sun, moon and stars come into view.

Again, to the human sense of sight when standing on earth, it *appears* as if these heavenly bodies rise above earth's horizon.

It also appears as if these bodies all rotate in space around earth.

So—to the untrained eye, it really does look as if the earth is a massive flat object.

And it really does appear as if earth is at the center, and the universe is geo-centric—with the sun, moon, planets and all stars rotating around it.

What counts are the *beliefs* that arose out of these illusions.

The most famous was, "Don't dare sail beyond the horizon of this flat earth, or you'll fall off."

Needless to say, peoples' acceptance of the beliefs acted like self-imposed barriers which were incredibly limiting.

Again, all due to illusion.

* * * * *

Here's the point of dredging up this old example.

Today we pride ourselves on being much more savvy, advanced and enlightened than the flat earth folks.

We don't like to think of ourselves as still capable of accepting illusions and ignorant beliefs.

Yet, unwittingly, we are.

What if exposing this other illusion were so significant and potentially freeing—it would make the old geo-centric universe breakthrough seem trivial?

What if you were not a mere passive observer in this—but an active participant?

* * * * *

To expose the illusion is not difficult.

All that's necessary is to stay open to seeing your present experience in a completely new way.

The illusion is gradually exposed as the following chapters walk through simple experiential noticing exercises drawn from everyday experience.

Many noticings deal with the five senses of sight, touch, sound, taste and smell.

In a new way, you'll experience how the senses seem to create illusory appearances.

This illusion is not anyone's fault—it's just how the senses function.

It will become obvious that this illusion has fooled us into believing there is a physical, material world of solid objects "out there."

There isn't.

The fact is, all of what appears as everyday experience really could be called *mental* instead of physical.

It's similar to a sleeping dream. A dream has no physical, solid items in it—it's all only mental—but when asleep it may *seem* physical and real.

All items we seem to sense—from bananas to bodies to earth—actually are just *perceptions*. They are not separate, solid objects.

They really are more like ideas or concepts, in a boundless, all-embracing universal consciousness or awareness.

As already noticed, this awareness literally is *alive*—the *living* substance in which all existing appears to go on.

Again, this is why boundless awareness could be called Life itself.

* * * * *

How will exposing this illusion affect today's current beliefs?

As said earlier, it is generally believed today that Life is only *on* planet earth.

Many are willing to admit the possibility that Life may be on other planets, too.

But notice something crucial here.

That still involves a belief of Life having to be *on* things—*on* physical planets.

The key word is "on."

The reason for this belief of "Life being on" is due to *another* belief.

It's the belief that Life is limited to being *inside* solid objects.

Supposedly, Life has to be inside human bodies, or animal bodies.

Life also is believed to be inside forms of vegetation such as plants and trees.

This is the illusory way in which the five human senses of sight, touch, hearing, etc. appear to portray the world.

To the human senses, it certainly *looks* as if Life is inside human, animal and plant forms.

And, of course, these things certainly appear to be *on* planet earth.

Admit it. This belief of Life having to be *on* earth and *in* objects seems so ingrained (like the flat earth) that it's rarely questioned by society.

The belief that Life is *on* earth is our current era's version of the *flat* earth.

* * * * *

Think of a sleeping dream you had recently, or imagine one now.

See the characters in the dream.

Say they appear to be outdoors, and trees appear in the dream.

When dreaming, the dream characters certainly *appear* animated, and even may talk and act intelligently.

But is there really any life contained *inside* those characters?

The dream characters are nothing but mental images, or perceptions—mere wisps of dream-like thought.

In the dream, there are no actual solid, physical bodies *there* that could contain life.

Nor are there any solid physical heads to those characters that could contain their seeming awareness, consciousness.

There equally are no solid physical trees or vegetation in the dream, in which any life could be.

Nor are the dream bodies and trees on a solid physical earth.

That may be how it appears when dreaming.

But when awake, it is clear there is no solid or physical stuff to anything in that dream.

* * * * *

Once the illusion is exposed, later chapters will begin to glimpse the fantastic implications of all this.

Its magnificence is inevitable after seeing through the false belief of Life being *on* earth.

To glimpse what this means, first consider what it meant to see through the belief of a *flat* earth.

The world and man's experience eventually opened up in so many ways it's indescribable.

Suddenly there was another side of the new round world, and new realms to explore.

Yet even with all this new freedom, notice something about all of that new-world experience.

It still was believed that the experience was occurring on a *physical* planet, in a limited material world of *physical* space and time.

What if Life and all experience really were *not* physical?

What if all Life really, truly, was like a state of infinite *imagination?*

What if Life really had none of those weighty limits of physical space, material objects and time?

It literally would leave none of those so-called physical limitations!

But the first step would be to *start* with Life as Life really is—and not be taken in by illusion, beliefs and limitations.

* * * * *

It took many years for the "round" earth to be generally accepted.

So the *limitations* of the old belief lingered.

Today is different.

In this apparent age of having instant information everywhere, there is no need to continue laboring under an old belief and a severely limited way of living.

The reason for using the old geo-centric universe example is that it's actually a helpful parallel.

Some of the noticings in these pages may seem radical at first, and bring up doubts.

That's only because they refute the currently popular *belief* of Life being *on* earth.

If doubts come up, simply notice how radical a round earth may have seemed at first, too.

* * * * *

Millions of books have been written since the era of Galileo, Copernicus and Columbus.

Whether it is realized or not, most of those books contain views that arose out of the new view of earth—as a tiny round physical planet floating in space.

What is the significance of this latest view—of Life's awareness being all-embracing of the universe and all there is?

In other words, what is the significance of earth and all things being mere perceptions—more like ideas or concepts in awareness, consciousness—and not physical objects in physical space?

Just making this one point clear is enough of a task for any book.

To then get into what it *means* is something else.

Millions of books can be written on this new basis also—and that's what is so exciting.

So this is just the tip of the iceberg—a humble beginning to notice this unlimited magnificence that Life already, effortlessly is.

* * * * *

12 Yes, We Have No Bananas

This chapter title is from a popular 1920's song of the same name. It happens to be perfectly appropriate here, as you will see.

Suppose you were buying a new home or expensive car.

You would ask questions.

Before agreeing to anything and making a deal, most likely you would look closely at all the details.

What about the details of the very Life you are?

You might want to look closely at what kind of deal *that* has been.

* * * * *

To begin seeing how the sensory illusion works, first look at how it normally appears.

The everyday world certainly does appear to consist of many solid, separate, physical objects.

Two such items would be this book, and the body now holding this book.

Other objects could be furniture near where the body now may be seated.

A shoe appears to be a type of solid object, too.

So do most everyday items—like a fork and spoon. And a cinder block, or a banana.

Trees and mountains appear to be objects.

On it goes.

Supposedly, the grand mother physical object of them all, is earth.

Strange as it may seem, that's the illusion.

It appears as if all these things are "out there" and separate from "you here" as the body.

It also appears as if these objects are separated from each other by physical distance, and have space in between them.

That's part of the illusion, too.

* * * * *

Like a good detective, closely examine the scene.

Notice every bit of evidence for this so-called physical world of solid objects.

For example, how can it even be said there seems to be a body here right now, holding a book and experiencing such a world?

First, notice how *it all depends on the five senses sensing it.*

There is a seeing, or visual sense of a world.

There can be a hearing of what goes on in a world.

There can be a touching or tactile feeling of a world.

There can be a smelling and tasting of it.

All evidence testifying to the so-called physical world of solid matter can be traced to the five senses.

This sensory evidence seems so powerful, it can be very convincing—and usually it is all that gets *noticed.*

That's only because other things have gone *unnoticed.*

* * * * *

To expose this sensory illusion, consider a basic everyday item.

It's a nice yellow banana, and you're eating it.

In daily living, did you ever notice why it is even believed there *are* such things as bananas?

In response to this, notice if a thought comes, "Wait a minute. It's not just a belief that there are bananas—it's a fact."

Okay, on what is this "fact" based?

Consider all the evidence there is for any banana's existence.

See for yourself how it is all based on the five senses.

What usually gets noticed first is a specific sight or *visual sensation*.

There is an image or appearance to any banana.

In this case, the image is one of basically yellow color.

Notice how the shape of this yellow image gives the banana its oblong appearance.

The yellow appears to be longer in one direction—the length—and less in width.

Looking closely, you notice all that's really being seen is *color.*

Visually, there also appears to be a slight curve to this image of yellow color.

This image of yellow shape is how a banana is visually distinguished from other items—such as a finger, or a flashlight.

This image or visual sensation of yellow is an essential piece of evidence for saying a banana is *there* in the first place.

* * * * *

Notice what happens simultaneously when experiencing the visual sensation or yellow image.

Sensations of touch, or various *tactile feelings* also can be experienced.

If a banana were held in the fingers, there would be a specific *feeling of texture* to its surface—perhaps smooth.

That *feel* is different from the feel of sandpaper, or a cotton ball.

There is another variation of tactile sensation, such as a *feeling of weight* when holding a banana. It's different from a brick.

Feeling-wise, there also is a sense of temperature—different from an ice cube.

The feelings supposedly are evidence of the banana's *solidity.*

In particular, notice these all are *feelings.*

* * * * *

Watch what happens when dealing with this tactile experience purely in terms of the feeling.

Don't automatically think of this banana-feeling experience in terms of two separate items—fingers *and* a banana.

Now deal *purely in terms of feeling*—deal with the tactile sensation alone.

Notice that if the eyes were closed, only one overall sensation or feeling would be experienced.

In terms of pure feeling only, there is no evidence of two items. No place can be noticed where "fingers" end and "banana" begins.

At all times, there is just one overall feeling being experienced.

There may be nuances to the feeling.

These are the texture, weight and temperature—but it is still all *feeling*.

Notice also how the feeling always would be changing if the banana were moved around.

The feeling is always passing, fleeting—shifting from one type of feel to another.

Notice closely that this feeling, in and of itself, is not considered a solid physical object—it's a mere feeling.

The general belief is that this feeling supposedly is a feeling *of* something else.

Supposedly this feeling is *from* a banana.

But notice all that's there is just a *feeling*.

* * * * *

Notice also the specific sense of *taste* with a banana if a bite were taken.

It is different from the taste sensation of a carrot.

There is a pleasant *scent* to a banana—different from gasoline.

There even may be a faint sense of *sound*—such as when the skin is peeled off, or when chewing.

Notice that even when chewing and swallowing—the soft texture in the mouth and throat really is another type of tactile *feeling*.

* * * * *

What happens when all of this sensory activity occurs at once?

Each of the five senses contributes its particular "aspect" of the banana to the overall experience.

There are visual color and shape, there are feelings, and taste, smell and sound.

When some or all of these five sensations are experienced, simultaneously there is the thought, "A banana is here."

Really notice that this same basic sensory process is what goes on all day long.

In a similar way, the five senses combine their activity in the experiencing of every single thing—from bananas to book reading to bike riding.

Even right now—there seems to be an experiencing of visual images and tactile feelings of what is called a book.

This same thing goes on moment by moment with every single item, every single day.

This sensory experience is how the so-called human mind experiences its entire world and *all* the things supposedly in it.

When the *particular combination* of banana-sensations occurs, it is what the mind or thought labels as "the experience of eating a banana."

* * * * *

Now look deeper.

Exactly what is the *substance* of the banana?

What does a banana *itself* consist of?

To not be fooled, look once more at all the evidence for a banana.

There is the visual sensation or image of yellow. There are tactile feelings. There is a taste sensation. There is a scent, and possibly a sound.

These sensations are *all* the evidence for saying a banana exists.

There is no *other* evidence.

Now leave the sensations a moment.

Ask yourself what the substance of the banana *itself* is—from which this sensory experience supposedly is coming.

What makes up the banana itself, *apart* from those sensations?

When you try to come up with what a banana is, entirely *separate* from the sensations, what happens?

You don't come up with anything.

And why don't you come up with anything?

Because there *isn't* anything!

There are only the sensations!

* * * * *

Look as long and as thoroughly as you want—the answer is always the same.

Sensations *alone* are the only "substance" for this entire experience.

There are not *both* the sensations *and* a separate banana.

There never is a solid banana-object "out there" having its own existence as a stand-alone physical item.

There is no separate object from which any sensations are coming.

At most, there is *only* an experience of some passing sensations— which would be an entirely "mental" phenomenon.

Go over this as often as necessary to be clear.

This means a so-called "banana" isn't really a solid physical object at all.

There is no such item with its own independent material presence.

At most, the so-called "banana" would consist only of sense perceptions or "mind stuff," like a *thought*, or a dream.

It might be more accurate to call it a "thought-banana"—because during this entire sensory experience, it is as if thought were saying, "A banana is here."

* * * * *

The same thing can be seen in reverse.

First *take away* the experiencing of those five mere sensations.

Now see if it is possible to claim a banana still is present.

It's not.

What does all this mean?

A "banana" as a separate, solid, physical item didn't go away anywhere.

No such separate object *ever was out there* in the first place!

Never has there been any such item having its own independent existence.

At first it may be best to just read these last few noticings several times. It is not necessary to actually hold a "banana" and try to "un-see" it. The sensory conditioning can seem strong and hypnotic, so it may be easier to be clear about this by first going through the examples without holding a "banana."

* * * * *

Until this illusion is exposed, naturally one is likely to think of "banana" as a solid, separate object.

Yet notice that it can't be said a mere image of yellow color is a separate *physical* object because again, an image would be only a perception, or mental.

There are not *both* the image and a separate object that is giving off the image. Always, there is *only* the image.

In the same way, a passing tactile feeling is just that—a mere *feeling*.

There is not also a permanent solid object anywhere from which the feeling is coming.

There are only fleeting, passing feeling-sensations which, in and of themselves, do not constitute a separate, static physical object.

Nor is a sensation of taste, or a sound or smell, in and of itself a separate, solid object.

The way the sensory illusion seems to work, it forms an *appearance* of being a separate, solid object "out there."

But the only substance for a "banana" would be a purely "mental" process, experienced only as perceptions, or thought.

There are not both the perceptions *and* a banana, as if a banana were separate.

There are only perceptions—*as* banana.

* * * * *

In the human scene, this noticing that so-called "objects" really are not separate physical items has been known to philosophers and sages for centuries.

Usually though, it is considered esoteric, or is limited to experts, which is why this is not more widely known.

On this basis, it also has been widely debated *where* all human experience seems to be occurring.

The debate has been whether all human experience is going on inside the mind or outside of the mind.

Actually, it's neither.

The banana is neither inside the mind nor outside the mind, but literally *would be* the mind itself in operation.

* * * * *

When the sensations associated with "banana" are experienced, it can't be said the sensations are produced by a banana that is outside the mind, or separate from thought.

No separate item is there to be outside, or to produce sensations.

Now look at this in reverse.

If it were not for that particular seeming "item" or "banana," that specific package of sensations wouldn't seem to occur either.

Those same sense perceptions would not be experienced with "onion."

The "banana" and that particular mental activity—the experiencing of those specific sense perceptions—seem to need each other.

It's because they would be opposite sides of the same coin.

This mental/sensory activity doesn't know *about* the banana, as if it were something separate. The mental activity *is* the banana.

Even the very discussion and explaining of this point—using the two words, *sensations* and *banana*—makes it sound as if there were two separate things.

There aren't.

It would be one phenomenon.

* * * * *

Here is the most important point to notice.

This isn't only about "bananas."

This same basic illusion applies to *all items* experienced in daily living!

It applies to cellphones, toothbrushes, computers, beer cans, birthday cake, dollar bills, automobiles, bodies—everything.

It even applies to the planet itself.

The significance and scope of the sensory illusion may seem staggering at first.

If it feels as if this has really "rocked the boat" it only would be because the seemingly age-old belief in a separate physical world has been "rocked."

So don't be surprised if, on seeing this, new questions come up—they should.

This is now an entirely new kind of world and Life.

* * * * *

13 What *Is* A Day, Anyway?

Don't kid yourself.

Even after seeing through this sensory illusion, conditioning still may make "objects" seem very real and solid.

It may be helpful at first to dis-assemble what appear as separate objects, such as the example with the "banana."

Have fun with it.

It always works the same for any so-called "object."

Always ask if it is possible to find a separate item apart from the sense-perceptions.

Ask if there is a stand-alone item there, having its own inherent substance, presence or existence, separate from the sensations or thought.

Always, the answer is the same—no separate object is there.

It only *seems* or *appears* as if there were.

Once this is clear, it is not necessary to keep dis-assembling objects.

* * * * *

When saying things are not physical but are "made out of thought"—exactly what does that mean?

The word *thought* can have different meanings.

Suppose your hands were now holding what appears as a banana.

In addition to that hand-held banana, suppose you also were to *think of* or *imagine* a second banana.

What is the difference between those two bananas? Are both the hand-held and imaginary bananas "made of thought"?

In one sense, yes. It depends on what is meant by *thought*.

First consider the hand-held banana.

The illusion that a solid-object "banana" is out there having its own separate physical existence, has just been seen through.

The "banana" actually would be sensory-only or mental—meaning it is not physical. To say "made out of thought" is just another way of saying "not physical."

The second banana (the one imagined) certainly *seems* more ethereal and non-physical than the hand-held banana.

It doesn't alter the fact that the hand-held banana is not physical.

This is why, in eastern philosophy, the hand-held banana is sometimes called a *gross thought* and the imagined banana is called a *subtle thought*.

After all, the imagined banana seems far more subtle or insubstantial compared to the hand-held.

Ultimately *both* would be non-physical perceptions, or thought.

One seems more physical and separate than the other—but that's the illusion.

* * * * *

Imagine having a dream.

A dream is merely mental images and "made out of thought," too.

Suppose the "you" in this dream were eating a banana.

It's not really a physical banana—but within the dream it seems so. It's really just a mental or dream-banana.

While eating your dream-banana, now suppose the dream "you" were to also *imagine* a second, chocolate-covered banana.

That imaginary chocolate banana also would be mental.

However, it would seem to be a more subtle type of banana.

It would be an imaginary mental form being thought up *within what is already a purely mental state*—the dream.

Within the dream, this imaginary chocolate banana might seem different or more subtle.

From within the dream it's not quite the same as the "gross" dream-banana being eaten by the dream "you."

Yet ultimately, everything is made of the same *one* stuff—the one dream.

In this sense, both "bananas" would be merely mental or thought.

It is similar in daily living.

What seem to be gross objects or thoughts and subtle thoughts both belong to what is really one overall mental state.

No wonder daily human experience sometimes is called "the waking dream."

* * * * *

Speaking of daily human experience, what is one of the most basic ways day-to-day living is experienced?

It is called just that—a *day*.

That which is considered to be "a day" is so accepted as a given, so taken for granted, it's almost never questioned.

What *exactly* is a day, anyway?

Did you ever notice that to even *say* there is such a thing as a day depends entirely on the five senses?

Notice something extremely revealing, which may not have been noticed before.

The entire experiencing of what is called a "day" is inseparable from what is seen, felt, heard, tasted or smelled.

First, take away all visual sensations—every single sight—that is experienced during a day.

That means *no* sights of waking up in bed, no sight of a sunrise or sunset, no sight of any clock, no sight of any rooms or a home, no car or workplace, and nothing in between.

No sights of outdoors, no planet, no sky, no sight of other people— not even your own body!

Without the visual sense, a lot of what is experienced as a "day" is suddenly gone, isn't it?

* * * * *

Next, suppose all *sense of touch* or *feel* experienced in a day were taken away.

That means no touches or feelings of a body being in bed or getting out of bed onto a floor. No feelings of walking around or touching things in a home or workplace, or outdoors.

There is not a single feeling of even the body itself! Not even scratching an ear or holding a book.

There is no feeling of a comfortable sofa, or car seat. No cell phone. No TV remote. No touching of food—whether by hand or mouth. No toothbrush. No touch of a bed again.

There are *none* of the countless other things it seems the body touches.

Next, take away all *sounds* experienced during a day.

No alarm clock. No sound of breathing. No sound of a phone, computer, radio or TV. No cars. No sound of wind. No music.

There are *no* sounds of voices. Not a single one—not even yours!

The "day" is disappearing pretty fast isn't it?

Then take away all smells, and all tastes, too.

Suddenly, the "day" no longer is there to be noticed!

The point is: There aren't the mere sensations of a day *and also* something separate called a day.

Sensations *are* the day.

* * * * *

Is it possible to notice *any* evidence of a day apart from sensations?

There might still be thoughts and emotions—but most of those, too, arise out of what has been sensed.

The illusion is that it is assumed there are the sensations—*and also* something separate called a "physical day" which the sensations are coming from. No!

Surprising as it may seem, a "day" would be entirely made out of thought, or a purely mental experience, too.

None of the experience is backed up by a physical world of separate objects.

Sensations don't tell you *about* a day, as if a day were something separate.

Mere passing sensations would be all there is *of* a day.

Notice something even more important.

Life's all-embracing pure *aliveness* is none of those sensations.

Life's invisible aliveness is not something seen, felt, heard, tasted or smelled.

So even if the *sense* of a day isn't being experienced, it doesn't mean Life is gone.

* * * * *

Notice some things about sensory experience and *time*—because a day would be time, too. They appear to be interwoven, inseparable.

It takes time to see, to experience a visual sensation—no matter how quick. Even the super-fast simple noticing of a blue sky takes a tiny amount of time.

It takes time to hear a sound. Time also seems to pass while experiencing tactile feelings, tasting and smelling.

The experiencing of sensations cannot be separated from time.

Now flip it around.

What is the only evidence that there even *is* time? Those same sensations.

Each day, an image of a yellow "disc" and a blue "sky" appears, which is nothing but a *visual sensation.*

Then there appears to be darkness, and lesser lights of "moon" and "stars"—all just more *visual sensations.*

In between are more *visual sensations* of clocks and wrist watches. There may be *sounds*—of alarm clocks, voices or church bells.

It's all mere sensory activity. Take it away, and there is *no* time.

What does it mean that there is no physical world from which it is coming—and it all would be *perceptions or "mental stuff" only?*

It means never are there days occurring in a separate physical world. Nor years. Nor have there been any centuries.

At most, there would be only "mental days" or dream-like days.

Sensations don't tell you *about* time as if time were separate.

The experiencing of sensations would be all there is *to* time itself.

* * * * *

On a clock, the second hand always is *moving, passing* the numbers on the clock face all day long.

Notice that time never seems to stop moving, passing on, to *be present*. If it did stop, it wouldn't be time!

Sensations always seem to move and change, too—passing on in time. Sensations, like time, never stop moving *to be present*.

Part of the illusion is that sensations do seem as if they *are* present.

The typical belief is that this book (or a banana) is a solid, *stationary* object—but it's really just constantly moving sensations.

Notice that each instant a visual sensation or feeling of "book" is experienced, it seems that particular image or feeling quickly moves on and is gone.

Where are the specific visual images experienced a few seconds ago when reading the top line on this page?

They've come and gone—replaced by images of reading *this* line, and so on. Each sensation is instantly replaced by a new one, and then another.

It's the same for all feelings, and all sounds, all tastes and smells, all day long. One moment they seem to be here, then they're gone.

They've been replaced by *these* images and feelings that seem to be experienced in this current instant.

Notice that thoughts and emotions come and go in the same way.

On and on this sensory flow seems to go, as what is believed to be "daily living" in a separate world.

Instead of there being objects and a world that are physically separate and solid—it's all more like mental fluid.

* * * * *

Notice some other things about the *way* sensory experience seems to occur.

See how the *way* is inseparable from *what* is experienced.

Say a blue sky is *what* is experienced.

The experiencing of blue color can't be separated from the *sight* of it, or the *way* it is experienced.

Without the visual sense, there could be no *image* of a blue sky.

Notice that some things, such as "orange juice" (the *what*) can be experienced in more than one *way.*

Obviously, that which is called "orange juice" can be experienced as a visual image.

Orange juice also can be experienced as a sense of taste—distinct from, say, the taste of coffee.

Of course, it can be experienced as a smell, touch and sound, too.

Compare the scent of orange juice to that of spaghetti sauce.

Notice how the tactile *feel* or *touch* of cool liquid in the mouth differs from the feel of a mouthful of hot popcorn. Even the *sound* from crunching a mouthful of popcorn is different from the sound of swallowing orange juice.

If that specific *way*—a visual sensation of orange colored liquid, a specific tangy sweet taste, cool touch, and smell were *not* experienced, it would not be possible to say orange juice (the *what*) even were there.

In other words, what happens when eliminating the *way* a thing is experienced?

You no longer have *what* is experienced.

* * * * *

Perhaps you're familiar with the example of looking down a long length of railroad tracks.

The tracks appear to come together in the distance.

To the visual sense, it looks as if the tracks touch, forming a point.

It appears as if the tracks form an actual *place* where they come in contact.

But when walking up to that seeming place on the tracks, there is no such place—only empty space between parallel tracks.

Of course, the parallel tracks never form an actual point or place anywhere.

If it were possible to build an endless length of straight railroad tracks, they would stretch parallel forever.

This appears to be true for *any* two parallel lines.

Notice how this reveals something else about the visual sense.

The visual sense makes it *appear* as if there are places—which are not really there as places.

So what does this mean when it comes to the appearance of *all places?*

* * * * *

The previous page showed that railroad tracks visually appear to form a point or place *that isn't really there.*

Now turn this illusory appearance around.

Start from the point end. Then work backwards.

In other words, what if every single point, every place the visual sense seems to see isn't really there as a place?

What if all points or places really are only like railroad tracks—countless parallel lines that extend endlessly, never really coming together to form a place?

What if all of daily experience with its *appearance* of all places, really is just parallel lines making an *illusion* of places?

Such points or places could be the tip of your nose. The tip of a finger. It could be the period at the end of this sentence—and all other points on this page.

This means *every* "place"—every point on every grain of sand—and *every single point everywhere else* on this planet and even throughout every point in so-called space.

What if none of those is *really* there? Why couldn't it be this way?

This applies to everywhere your body appears to have ever gone.

It even applies to the body itself as it appears to sit here holding this book—for the body is a kind of place, too. So is the earth on which it appears to rest.

All of them would be just a lot of appearing points or places.

If every single point on your body, on earth, and throughout the universe really isn't there as that spot—then what *is* there?

Only Life's infinite awareness.

* * * * *

All of daily experience is like the two sides of a coin.

Experienced from one side, the "world" seems to be one of material objects.

Some of these objects are called bananas, books, bodies, and glasses of orange juice.

What about when experienced from the other side of the coin—as sensations?

The "world" can just as readily be said to consist *merely* of colors, feels, sounds, smells and tastes.

You can't have one side of the coin without the other.

It seems that in everyday living, only one side of the coin gets most of the attention.

It's the side that mistakenly sees things as separate physical objects instead of as mere sense perceptions, or "mental."

What happens when closely noticing both sides of this coin with equal interest?

It becomes clear that sensations don't provide information *about* the world, as if the world were separate.

Sensations *are* the world.

The so-called world is *only* sensations, perceptions—nothing more.

* * * * *

When not fooled by sense appearances, there naturally is an appreciation for the immediacy and directness of all Life.

The fact that there really is nothing physical means *nothing is physically separate from anything else.*

Again, it's similar to how there is no physical distance separating things in a sleeping dream.

As the saying goes, there really is no "out there" out there!

It only appears that way.

The flip-side of there being no physical separateness or distance is "closeness" or immediacy.

This immediacy applies to what appears to be the *entire universe.*

Even a seemingly vast stellar universe suddenly is transformed—from intimidating to *intimate.*

It means Life's awareness, being alive here, now, is the very substance of all that exists!

That is something worth pondering.

There really never is the thought *of* a world—as if there were the thought *and also* a world as something separate "out there."

There is only thought "right here"—which appears *as* a world.

Never has there been any physical separation in Life.

It is all this *one* Life.

* * * * *

It's worth emphasizing the extent to which this immediacy or intimacy is the case for all so-called items.

It applies to every single seeming "object" in daily human experience!

It applies to home, workplace, streets, car, outdoors, food, friends and enemies.

It means this thought-state never *thinks about* things.

It literally *would be* all things.

This thought-state doesn't travel to, or think in terms of separate places.

It literally *would be* all "places."

When the blue sky is effortlessly noticed right here, now—it isn't that this noticing knows something *about* a sky and universe that have their own separate existence.

This very perceiving here, now, literally *is all there is of the sky and universe*!

It really is not physically distant—because thought is not distant.

* * * * *

14 It's Only A *Sense* Of A Body

While sensory appearances may be illusory, this does not mean *Life itself* is illusory.

Life's aliveness definitely is real and present.

It's just that the way the senses make everyday experience *appear* as separate, is not the way things really are.

This also does not mean the senses are intentionally trying to deceive.

This just seems to be their nature.

The senses by themselves don't know anything.

So they don't know to deceive anyone.

With noticing, there is no attempt to destroy or change illusory appearances.

Appearances are simply *seen through*.

* * * * *

Notice what general human belief always has said about the body and world.

The body generally is believed to be a solid object with a mind, consciousness, or awareness inside it.

Supposedly, this mind or awareness is inside a physical brain.

And, supposedly, the five senses deliver information inside, about what is believed to be a separate, physical world "out there."

But what if a body really is no different from a "banana"?

What if a body really is not a solid physical object either?

Then it couldn't be said awareness is inside a body.

There would be no solid object *there* to put anything inside of.

* * * * *

Examine the body slowly, like a "banana."

The prevalent belief would say, "Of course the body is a solid object. I can touch a leg with a finger and *feel* the solidity."

That belief comes from never looking beyond surface appearances.

The mistake is, body is *assumed* to be a solid object feeling itself.

So deal with this feeling of solidity first, and see what's really there.

What evidence can be found to be the *substance* of "body"?

When "finger" touches "leg" there seems to be a visual image and a feeling, yes.

But that's *all* there ever is.

There is not the feeling *and also* a separate solid leg from which the feeling comes. There is only a feeling.

When you try to find some other substance for a leg in addition to the mere feeling, you can't. Nothing *else* is there.

Notice the so-called "solidity" is just like when feeling the "solidity" of a "banana."

There aren't *both* a mere tactile feeling and *also* a separate solid banana from which the feeling is coming.

There is *only* a passing feeling—nothing else.

It's exactly the same when feeling any body part.

The only substance that ever can be found is a passing feeling.

A mere fleeting, passing feeling does not constitute a separate solid, static object.

* * * * *

When looking for other evidence of "body," what else is there?

There also seem to be visual images, of what is supposedly the "body" itself.

The images are called legs, torso, arms and other body parts.

Again, what is the mistake here?

The mistake is the *assumption* there are the images of "body" *and also* a separate solid object that is giving off those images.

No. There aren't both the images *and* a separate body-object that is giving off the images. Always, there are only mere images.

Seen this way, "body" is just passing colors and passing feelings.

A thought may come, "Body is flesh and bones."

Okay, but what would flesh and bones really be? Nothing but more sensations—also just images and feelings.

If a doubt remains, stop reading right now and find some other substance for a solid body beyond mere passing feelings or images.

It can't be done.

It is the same for all other sensations of "body," too.

This includes all sounds of "body" such as talking and breathing. The *only* evidence is sounds—there is no evidence of a separate solid object that is giving off the sounds.

It also applies to all smells and tastes. There aren't these mere sensations *and* an object.

The only "substance" to the whole experience of "body" is just a passing *flow* of un-solid sensations or thought-perceptions.

This means "body" is more like *mental fluid,* not physically solid.

* * * * *

See the "body" as it appeared to be sitting here just a few moments ago, when reading the previous page.

Notice that it already would be just an image in thought.

Now try to see body reading the next page, a few moments from now. It, too, would be just an image in thought, or imaginary.

In both cases, there is no physical solidity to that thought-image "body." It has no physical weight, no hardness or solidity.

Notice "body" right this moment, as it appears to read this line.

In this instant, body sure *seems* to be solid stuff.

Now lift one hand off the book a moment and wave it. Then put the hand back.

Right now, in *this* instant, where is the waving of the "hand" and feeling of the "book" from a few seconds ago?

Those sensations also are gone—and now are thought-images, too.

All those feelings and images of "body" already have passed on, having been instantly replaced by sensations being experienced in *this* current moment.

And the instant the sensations in *this* moment seem to be experienced, then they seem to be gone and replaced, too.

The point is, at any given moment as "body" *seems* to be sitting as a stationary object—it's really not.

At any time, all there is to "body" is this non-stop flow of mere passing sensations, constantly moving on, never stopping to *actually be present* as solid permanent stuff.

This constantly moving sensory fluid *always* is the only status of "body"—as well as everything else in daily living.

* * * * *

This sensory flow is like the movement of frames on a movie film.

Of course, a film contains many similar still images in a sequence. Each is a new one, moving at rapid speed through the projector.

The frames move and change so fast, the viewer's eye can't detect it—so it appears as if a single, constant image were on the screen.

Everything sensed in daily experience is like that.

Rapidly changing new sensations are all there is of *every seeming item* supposedly experienced during a day.

As each instant of sensing is constantly passing or moving on, so this "book" and the entire "day" itself always are moving on, too.

It seems some items aren't moving because the senses themselves are moving at the same speed as what they are sensing.

Imagine flying cross country on a jet, sipping coffee in your seat.

The jet, your body, and the coffee all are moving at the exact same speed. From inside the jet, the coffee doesn't appear to be moving. It isn't sloshing all over.

When down on the ground and looking up at the jet, the coffee definitely *is* moving—at about 450mph across the sky!

All there would be to any so-called thing or "place" is nothing but this constantly moving, mere mental fluid.

Daily experience really *is* like a dream.

Life's invisible presence, aliveness, is *not* a dream—because it is not any of this moving activity.

* * * * *

Notice what appears to go on all during the day.

It starts the moment the "body" appears to awaken in "bed."

There isn't this sensory mental state *and* any form of experience apart from it.

The sensory flow would be all there is of the bedroom, the bed, and even the body that appears to be in the bed.

It's all one fluid thought-state; a kind of sensory soup.

There is no separate, solid furniture, no house that is physically separate.

There are no separate family members, no separate pets, no separate planet.

None of it is solid physical items having a separate existence on their own.

It's the same when buying food, buying new clothes, a car, or any other thing.

It's really a matter of buying a package of sensations—not physical objects.

It all would be merely a mental or thought-state buying into a certain thought-pattern that it seems to resonate with.

See it for what it really is, not for what it *appears* to be.

* * * * *

Like a movie screen, Life's present aliveness never moves, never comes or goes—no matter how much sensory movement seems to be superimposed on it.

With all of this talk of the senses, don't lose sight of how there also seems to have been a huge transition from the earlier chapters.

It has been a transition *away* from these more obvious moving sensory forms such as visible images, touches and sounds.

Now there is a *feeling* or *being alive as* the invisible calm presence of Life's all-embracing aliveness.

Notice this.

Notice also that Life's all-inclusive aliveness is *not* an out-of-body experience.

Rather, Life's alive presence always is fully present as "everywhere"—even throughout where the body *appears* to be.

It's as if the appearance of the body is superimposed on Life's complete presence, the way movie characters are just images superimposed on the completely present screen. All the while, perfect Life is what's really present.

* * * * *

The noticings of an un-solid "body" and "matter" are simply saying the same thing that is taught in high school chemistry class.

They would call it un-solid atoms and energy.

Now it's just seen from a different angle.

The point is, Life itself *couldn't* be limited to being inside a body that's *not there* as a static object to have Life inside of it.

This doesn't mean one will misuse body because it is not physical.

It's just that the body is not the way it appears by way of the senses—not separate or made of solid matter.

Notice that just because what appears to be a visible solid body isn't really that way, nothing has changed with Life's invisible aliveness, the real *You*.

Life most definitely is present, is real and is not going anywhere.

It always is calm, serene—as immovable, all-embracing aliveness.

Body hasn't gone anywhere either. It still appears to be here, available to be used freely.

All that is "gone" is a false belief of being a physical, mortal body.

No such state ever was real anyway.

This also is not meant to minimize what appear as current medical practices for treating a "physical body."

These seem essential, and may continue for an indefinite period.

However, this doesn't keep Life's gently alive awareness from being all presence and all-embracing of all.

* * * * *

Questions may linger about awareness not being inside the body.

One question might go like this: "If Life's awareness, consciousness, is not inside the body, then why am I not still aware if the body is unconscious or under heavy anesthesia?"

"If awareness is not *inside* the body, awareness should be unaffected and still functioning if those things happen to the body."

Look carefully at what is being referred to.

Exactly what is it that changes or is gone, when the body goes from being conscious to unconscious? What becomes "un"?

When "conscious," there is an experiencing of sight, sound, feeling, taste, and smell, as well as thinking and emotions.

Notice closely that these all are *sensations* or body-mind activity.

Sights, sounds, feelings, etc. and even thoughts—all would be noticeable, *observable forms.*

When it seems the body is "unconscious," it would be the experiencing of those *observable forms* that stops or becomes "un."

Now notice that Life's pure awareness, invisible aliveness, is not any of those observable forms to begin with.

Life's invisible awareness itself *never is observable*—not even when "conscious." It never appears in any form.

So even though the observable forms are not observable during "unconsciousness"—it doesn't mean Life's un-observable alive presence has gone.

It is only the activity of the human body-mind, or mere "sensory consciousness" that stops.

It is not Life's infinite invisible aliveness, awareness.

* * * * *

If you have ever given much thought to questions like the preceding one, you may have noticed another.

"If awareness, Life's alive presence, is not inside a body and is present even when the body is "unconscious"—then why isn't there any memory of the experience?"

Sometimes there *is* a memory of the experience, as documented in many near-death experiences.

But memory of an experience is not the real point.

Notice exactly what memory is.

What is called a memory is just a *thought*.

Memory would be some kind of projected mental image.

But Life's pure awareness, invisible alive presence, is not any kind of thought or image. It is not thinkable.

Awareness cannot be projected in thought as a memory because pure awareness cannot be reduced to any thought form that could be projected.

What's more, Life's awareness always is present-tense only.

It is not possible to have a memory of awareness because it is not possible to have a memory of the present.

It's impossible to remember the present because it's never something past—it's only present.

* * * * *

15 What On Earth Have We Been Believing?

It sure seems as if the "body" walks on solid ground every day.

Yet it almost never is questioned if ground *really is* solid ground!

What does an experience of "walking on solid ground" actually consist of?

What is all the evidence that can be found to be the substance of "earth"?

There is a visual sensation—images of what is supposedly ground.

There is a feeling sensation—supposedly "feet" on a massive base.

Perhaps there also are some sounds, or some smells.

But those mere sensations are *all* the substance there is to the entire experience.

When you try to find something in addition to those mere sensations, some additional substance to be a separate "earth," you can't.

There aren't those mere images and feeling sensations *and also* a solid, separate earth-object from which the sensations come.

There *never has been* any such separate earth-object!

Always, all there would be to the experiencing of "earth" is nothing but images of color and passing feelings.

Nothing else is *there*.

* * * * *

Peter Francis Dziuban ~

By now it should be obvious.

How then could Life be limited to being *on* an earth?

There is no solid object earth *out there* for Life to be on!

That which is called "earth" actually would be just an appearance *in* Life—nothing more than sense perceptions in infinite Life's boundless awareness or perceiving.

A bunch of mere passing sense perceptions is not a static physical object on which anything could be put or located.

At most, the "body" would be mere sense perceptions, too.

A bunch of mere perceptions cannot be physically located *on* other perceptions—because nowhere is there anything physical.

Sometimes the realization of this is said to be "the end of the earth" as prophesied in the Bible and other traditions.

To say, "the end of the earth" really means what?

It would be the end of a *belief* that there is a material object and world physically separate from that which is doing the perceiving.

Notice this hasn't done away with "earth"—it still appears to be right here.

In fact, now it is more intimate than ever!

Most importantly, this "end of earth" is not the end of *Life.*

If anything, it seems to be a beginning of a brand new way of experiencing earth and Life!

Notice also that, to Life itself, nothing has changed.

Life *always* is this way—it just has gone unnoticed.

* * * * *

Countless new books could and will be written on the significance of a perception-earth, instead of a separate object-earth.

What are just a few things this means?

This means nothing is occurring on an enormous physical planet occupying space—for there is no such object to occupy space!

Only solid physical objects could occupy space.

To fill or occupy physical space, all seeming "objects," including earth, would need to have physical length, width and height—or, in the case of earth—circumference or physical distance.

But physical distance is exactly what a purely mental state *does not have*!

As there is no separate object earth, no such thing as physical ground or space—there is nothing on which Life's infinite alive presence could be grounded!

It may *appear* the body is grounded and subject to gravity—but that's the illusion—and it is not Life's boundless alive presence.

Never are you alive in a *place*.

It is within the boundless Life You are, that all "places" appear. And at most, they would be only "mental places," not physical.

* * * * *

Life itself simply cannot be physically or geographically localized any *where*—because that type of physical "where" no longer exists.

No such things as physical or geographical locations ever really *did* exist.

That was the illusion.

Rather, the boundlessness of Life's awareness itself is all the "where" there is.

Life's awareness just seems to *float* as its own un-grounded-ness.

It is not even *in* a universe.

The entire universe would be merely a thought-appearance within aware Life!

Begin to notice what it feels like to be utterly without end, completely unlimited, as this alive, aware perceiving.

What is it to be un-confinable, un-restrain-able, *as alive stuff?*

* * * * *

In seeing that "earth" is not a separate, solid object on which Life could be located, notice what seems to have happened.

Nothing actually changed with "earth" because *there never really was* any such separate object.

Nothing has changed with Life either.

Life always has been all-embracing of all.

The only change that seems to have occurred is a falling away of how earth and Life had been *mistakenly perceived.*

The seeming change has come due to a transition away from perceiving by way of a body and sensory illusion.

Now the perceiving is from Life's pure awareness or intelligence—not illusory appearances.

For some, the notion of a universal consciousness or awareness can be an intimidating, hard-to-get-your-head-around idea. That's the reason for all this "Life is not on earth" discussion.

It's simply another way of saying the same thing.

To say, "Life is not *on* earth—rather, earth is *in* conscious Life" crystallizes the idea in a new way. It distills a sometimes difficult paradigm into plain, attention-getting language.

Suddenly, an idea that had been perceived as esoteric becomes something everyone wants to know about.

* * * * *

What else does it mean that all apparent "earth activity" really would be just dream-like thought, or *mental* ?

This doesn't mean the body is supposed to instantly start floating around everywhere.

Just begin noticing what it means to see through an illusion of being *on*.

There really is not a *physical* law known as gravity—because there is nothing physical.

There really are not two separate physical objects—earth and body—to have one exerting a gravitational pull on the other.

If anything, the experience of gravity, too, would be merely a mental state.

That means gravity really would be only a state of thought, a belief— not a physical law.

While this may be clear, it doesn't mean one is instantly living one hundred percent on that basis, and no longer has any physical sense of a body.

So this is not suggesting that any body should jump off a building to prove gravity is only a belief!

* * * * *

Suppose in a sleeping dream, your body was an Olympic diver.

The dream "body-you" goes for the gold medal, leaping off the high dive board.

Is there really a physical body in that dream, doing any diving?

When splashing into the cool dream-water after a perfect dream-dive—was any *physical wetness* actually there?

In the dream, the pool appears to be 20 feet deep to enable such high dives. Is there actually any *physical depth* of 20 feet in that dream?

Of course, the dream-pool has no physical depth, length or width, and no physical water.

But from within the dream it sure seems so.

The onlookers appeared to cheer from the grandstand at poolside. Was there even any physical distance separating pool and poolside?

The dream onlookers were not solid objects, and not separated from each other by physical space.

Nor was there any physical distance separating the "diver-you" from "them"!

There isn't so much as a millionth of an inch of *physical* distance in that dream.

Were there three types of physical substance—dry ground, water, and bodies?

Or was there only one pseudo "substance"—the dream?

* * * * *

The dream-like illusion of daily experience actually is no different from the pool dream.

It makes no difference how physical, separate and solid things may seem or appear.

When not identifying as one of the characters in a dream—but as Life's all-embracing awareness—what's different?

Isn't there only *one Life present* for what appears as all the characters and the whole picture?

There may appear to be many body-images, but there is only one Life or awareness present.

There is only *one actually alive substance* wherein they all appear.

* * * * *

Imagine having another dream. This time your dream-body is moving to another city.

In this dream, your dream-body is packing things in large cardboard boxes.

One box appears to be 3 ft. long, 3 ft. wide, and 3 ft. high, or deep.

You visually see and carefully measure the three *dimensions* to be sure your items will fit inside the dream-box's *space*.

The dream-box also is on the floor in the center of the dream-room because, again, its three dimensions take up so much *space*.

Now suppose you suddenly awaken from the dream.

Was that dream-box really 3 ft. long, wide, and deep in terms of physical space or distance?

It seemed to be, according to the dream sense, but the box did not have three physical dimensions of length, width and height.

The "box" actually was un-dimensional.

There was *zero physical distance* from the front of the "box" to the back.

The "box" was space-less.

In the dream it felt like cardboard, and seemed to fill space. But that was all illusory dream-sensations.

The entire dream really was just space-less, dimension-less mental images and feelings.

* * * * *

Next, suppose the body now holding this book appeared to be packing a "real" box for moving.

That "box" actually would be no different from the dream "box."

All there would be to that "box," too, is just space-less mere images and feelings.

Even the "move" is distance-less, and not really to another distant *physical* city or location.

All seeming "locations" would be just more sensations, too.

It's merely a move or *shift* to a new state of mental fluid—to a new package of sense perceptions.

That's because all there would be to it all is *just* sensations or thought.

You do not live in a three-dimensional world—it only *appears* as if a three-dimensional world is within You.

* * * * *

Think of a teaspoon.

Now think of countless starlit galaxies, appearing to stretch endlessly across deepest space.

Which is bigger and has more depth—the thought of teaspoon, or the thought of galaxies?

Neither.

Both take up the same amount of physical size, or space—none.

All there would be to both is mere *thought*.

Notice again that thought has no physical characteristics, no physical size.

In a state of thought, nothing is physically larger, smaller, separate, or distant from anything else.

No matter how hypnotic it may seem or appear, daily experience is no different.

* * * * *

Imagine watching an outer space movie.

On the movie screen is an image of a starship, apparently hurtling through huge galaxies speckled with distant stars.

The starship disappears into what seems to be the endless depth of distant space.

Now what if *you're the movie screen?*

That image of deep space appearing on you actually has zero physical depth or distance to it.

Regardless of the *appearance* of vast, deep space—everything is always "right here" on you, the space-less, depthless screen.

If one is fooled and judges only by the apparent images, there appears to be movement over seemingly great distances.

As the screen itself, you never move anywhere.

Likewise with the appearance of daily experience.

It makes no difference how spatial or full of distance it may *seem*.

All any experience ever really is, is just so much distance-less thought.

It always is appearing "right here" within, or on, Life's ever-present "screen" of alive awareness.

When mistakenly identified as a "body" it seems this "body-you" has moved all over the place.

When identified as Life's ever-present "screen" of perceiving, it is clear that all-embracing infinite Life itself never has moved an inch— just as the screen never moves during a movie.

* * * * *

Notice something about what is called The Big Bang—the currently popular scientific theory for the origin of the universe and space.

Scientific measurements today indicate beyond doubt that the universe appears to be *expanding*. The theory is that this apparent expansion today is a result of an explosion from long ago.

To see how it works, imagine starting from the size of the universe today, and looking backward through time.

It is reasoned that, if the expanding universe has reached a certain size today, then millions of years ago it was much *less* expanded.

And millions of years before that, it was much smaller still. And so on—all the way back to the so-called explosion or big bang which supposedly caused all the expansion.

This is how things appear from a so-called *physical* perspective.

But that's like looking at only one side of a coin. Now notice the other side.

Absolutely all this evidence of a universe, along with all its so-called expansion, is *inseparable from sensing or thought*.

All evidence, *all* measurements, and *all* conclusions have been obtained entirely by way of something seen, heard, or touched.

Even all the so-called scientific measurement devices, such as radio telescopes, or sophisticated computers and their programs—these, too, really consist *only* of sensations, thought.

There simply is no objective, spatial, physical universe that exists on its own *separate* from this sensing state of thought.

So if speaking of expansion—it can just as readily be said this expansion of a "universe" is as much an expansion of *thought*.

They just would be the two different sides of the same coin.

* * * * *

Notice again how a movie *appears* to involve movement across great distances. Yet none of the movie ever moves off the screen.

If one gets caught up in the movement of those images and their story, it may *seem* one has moved along with them (all the while sitting still in the audience).

It's similar in daily experience.

Staggering as it may seem, never has the body-thought holding this book-thought ever traversed even an inch of *physical* distance.

What *seems* to be movement across distance really would be what?

It would be just mental movement, the hypnotic movement of dream-like thought or space-less sense perceptions.

This seeming mental movement actually does not involve physical size, nor extension into physical space—even though it sure *seems* to. Once again, that's the illusion.

Meanwhile, the infinite "screen" of Life's aliveness never moves.

It only seems there is movement to the extent there is identification with the *moving sensations*—instead of as *un-moving, all-embracing awareness.*

Thoughts may come, "No movement in daily experience? What about my aching feet from all the marathons I've run?"

"What about my airplane travel—all around the planet?"

"What if I were an astronaut, and had traveled to outer space?"

All those experiences, too, would consist only of sense perceptions or thought—never involving *separate* physical objects or places.

You are the ever-present "screen" of *Life's aliveness*—not a constantly moving character that appears on it.

* * * * *

16 Life Itself Is Not A Dream

Notice what it means to see a dream for the *dream* it is.

It shows that *you* are not a dream.

It shows that you are not dreaming.

If you *were* the dream or dreaming—then the dream would be reality to you—and not a dream.

You would be entirely under the dream's influence—and incapable of seeing the dream *as* a dream.

* * * * *

Some of these noticings may have shaken up some mistaken beliefs about "body" and "world."

If it seems that way, notice something again about Life itself.

Life's simple, clear perceiving is still right here, *perfectly present as ever.*

Life itself is not shaken up.

Life's capacity to perceive and unconditionally include an entire universe in its silent Love hasn't been budged one bit.

Only a state of thinking—with its beliefs and assumptions based on illusion—may seem to have been shaken up.

The difference is that now there no longer is bondage to illusion and mistaken beliefs.

* * * * *

You're a train engineer.

You look ahead down the railroad tracks and they appear to come to a point in the distance.

Judging only by the sensory evidence, the train surely will jump the tracks.

Because you know it is an illusion and *see through* the appearance, you don't suddenly stop the train.

It is not necessary to think strenuously to try to change the appearance—and "un-see" the tracks coming to a point.

Nor do you try to manifest parallel lines, or turn to the universe to provide them for you!

And you don't keep saying, "This is only an illusion, a dream!"

You just proceed as normal—all the while clear that the appearance is not real.

* * * * *

Notice also if doubts arise: "This hasn't *changed* anything. All items still appear to be solid objects—such as this book—it looks the same as ever."

What happened when the belief in a flat earth was eventually discarded?

The same sensory appearance of flatness continued to appear.

The difference was that the appearance was seen or perceived from a different perspective and no longer taken at face value.

The false appearance no longer acted as a restriction or barrier.

Gradually there was a falling away of all the limiting beliefs about what lay beyond the horizon.

Now, the same thing will happen with the current belief of Life being only *on* a round physical object earth.

All those limits eventually will appear to fall away, too.

They seem to have arisen out of the illusion of a separate physical world of earth, space and time being "out there."

Such limiting beliefs also must dissolve—just as a sleeping dream cannot resist dissolving once you are fully awake.

* * * * *

Notice what happens when awakening from a sleeping dream.

Most of the time the dream simply is seen as a dream—and you go about daily affairs as normal.

If the dream were a nightmare, awakening might bring relief.

If the dream were enjoyable, there might be a longing or regret after the dream ended. But it would be a waste to continue regretting because it's clear the enjoyment wasn't real anyway.

What *doesn't* happen upon awakening?

You don't feel guilty or foolish about having been temporarily asleep and taken in by the dream.

You also never get angry and go back and try to destroy the dream—because it's not anywhere to destroy.

Most of all, you don't waste time telling yourself all day long, "It was only a dream!"—because you now are too busy living your *awake* life!

It is the same in daily experience.

You stay awake.

It is clear that the *appearance* of daily living doesn't really consist of many—many objects, many separate people, and many places.

There really is only *one*—one all-embracing Life.

Affairs are conducted as normal, but the *apparent* experiences no longer have the influence they did when believed to be separate.

* * * * *

If any of these noticings seem surprising or shocking, just continue to notice why it seems that way.

As said earlier, it would be only because there has been a departure from a prior pattern of limited, conditioned thinking.

It's similar to when the old geo-centric universe thinking had to be discarded, too.

What has been noticed is "outside the box" of the general belief structure.

You now are way beyond "thinking outside the box."

You now are permanently outside of all so-called boxes, because as Life's infinite awareness you are *outside of all thinking*.

You are the infinite awareness that gives rise to all thinking.

Now that thinking is driven by Life's intelligence, oneness—not illusion.

Notice if there is a feeling of, "Well, at least when *inside* the box, things were familiar. It was comfortable. This is a bit strange."

Notice that this, too, would be just another *thought*.

Meanwhile, Life's awareness, the real You, is as perfectly and effortlessly present as ever.

Might as well get used to this because, as Life's unlimited awareness— you actually *never were* in any box.

* * * * *

When seeing through an illusion of physical objects and physical distance, many brand new things are noticed.

One of them is that the entirety of what exists is so *immediately* present here, now, it is indescribable!

Just stop to let in what it means that the "three-dimensional world of space" actually is space-less, just as a dream is space-less.

That's *immediacy.*

It means Life's state of perceiving *present right here* has nothing beyond itself.

There really is no physical extension through any space; there is no distance in which separateness or a "beyond" could exist!

So, again, *nothing is separate from anything else*!

That is the illusion that has been seen through.

Nothing is separating *the whole of Life* from all of itself right here!

All of Life has to be *here*—for there is no "where" else.

All of Life is here—not as person or body, and not in a physical place—but here *as invisible, all-inclusive aliveness.*

* * * * *

Notice it would be just a speculative *thought* trying to say there is more of Life elsewhere.

And even that thought would be going on only right here.

This is it!

Being this Life is neither a personal ability nor personal responsibility.

It is one hundred percent Life's "job" to be this—and Life never fails.

If one judges only by sensory illusion, it may appear as if "other bodies" can say the same thing.

But notice that those "others" really would be just perceptions, thought-images, also appearing in *this* one Life.

They are no different from the body now holding this book—for this body, too, would be just perceptions appearing in *this* one Life.

Life itself does not belong to any *body,* but "belongs" entirely to Life itself.

Life itself is the only one that can be Life itself—and Life is fully, perfectly being itself.

* * * * *

202

Begin to notice something about day-to-day worries and problems, and general unhappiness.

Ask yourself how much of it has arisen out of a mistaken belief.

It's the mistaken belief that there is a weighed-down "body-object-you" that is separate from Life.

This "you" must struggle and fend for itself—because it is believed to be just one of countless other separate objects, located on a very weighty physical world in which everything has to fend for itself.

This separate "body-you" is constantly forced to plot and plan how it will succeed in competition with "others."

It is because a "body-you" supposedly has been taught this by a society that seems to have been laboring under the same belief.

Begin to notice how much stress and unhappiness seem to have occurred in daily living because of that belief.

Yet all the while, there never really has been *that* kind of world.

So notice how some of those problems can be released instantly.

While many others may not be so quickly let go of—at least they can be seen in a new light.

There really never has been that kind of Life.

Life's all-embracing aliveness never is at war with its own aliveness.

Life's pure aliveness never is poor, or diseased.

Such things seem to arise out of beliefs due to sensory illusion.

You are not now under that spell.

This is an entirely *new* kind of Life.

* * * * *

Life's awareness is unlimited—all there is of all there is.

As it is *all*, Life cannot be confined to any one, single "where."

This is the great difference between identifying as Life's awareness which is *all*—or as a mere body.

As Life's awareness, there is nothing to fear.

Nothing can come in and threaten from outside. Why?

Because the unlimited *allness* of Life itself leaves no such thing as an outside.

That's what *all* means.

If Life co-existed with something besides itself that was outside itself, Life wouldn't be *all*.

The endless total presence of the one Life itself leaves nothing else besides Life from which a threat could come.

* * * * *

Notice something again about pure Life itself.

Life, or aliveness, is *actively being alive* right now.

It is *presently* being alive.

Be still a moment. Relax.

Without thinking, silently feel or simply *be alive as* Life's alive presence.

Again, this alive presence has no physical or sensory qualities.

Life's pure aliveness doesn't even have any conceptual or mental qualities.

Yet here Life's aliveness is, being invisible and un-think-able, yet *distinctly*, alive, aware.

When consciously present as what You truly are—Life's pure aware presence—then what still appears by way of the senses may appear more beautiful and harmonious than ever.

It's because the experience no longer is being mis-seen by way of illusion, and now is being perceived by Life as it truly is.

* * * * *

As Life's awareness has no physical qualities, it has no weight, no feeling of heaviness.

Life's pure awareness cannot be said to weigh *anything*.

This non-heaviness is an almost indescribable lightness.

Be alive as this alive lightness right here.

Notice this is the true essence of the one being alive here, now.

Notice how this alive lightness is *always* present and available.

It is not something that is available *to* you—this lightness *is* You.

Notice this aliveness always is "on" or functioning, "alive-ing."

Where is it written that one can't be alive as this effortless lightness all day long?

After all, this is what Life itself is doing—and who else is being alive?

* * * * *

Just as Life's pure, simple aliveness has no weight or heaviness, it has no physical *solidity*.

This presently alive awareness has no seeming hardness to it, the way a "brick" seems to.

Feel, *be alive as*, how incredibly un-solid or "soft" this presently alive awareness is.

Feel again how Life's pure aliveness has no physical thickness or density. It has less hardness than air.

If anything, Life's present aliveness is an utter "softness" that is soft beyond even the softest of feathers.

What is it to fccl that this softness is actually alive?

Be alive as this unspeakable softness.

Notice this softness never is *not* soft, never not alive.

Notice that when *alive as* Life's softness, there is no wall, no border where softness stops being purely soft.

It is *endlessly* soft.

Notice that there is no limited physical quantity of this softness.

You can be alive as softness as much as you want, and softness never runs out, never goes away.

Softness can't go away. Life's all-embracing softness is *all there is*.

This alive softness always is immediately available wherever You are—because it is *what* You are.

* * * * *

Pure, raw Life is fully engaged in being *presently alive* only.

Pure aliveness doesn't cling to thoughts or project thoughts.

Only *thinking* seems to cling or project.

To identify only with thinking, emotions or sensations instead of *as aliveness* is to be "off" of Life.

From the standpoint of Life itself—Life only can be freely, presently *alive.*

Life itself carries no mental or emotional weight—but is naturally light, buoyant.

It need not make effort to be present.

Present Life is simply, spontaneously alive—totally without a border.

Life never has another state besides itself, thus never knows fear.

Life never looks outside itself for validation or a sense of worthiness— for the one Life has no other besides itself to look to.

Life is complete in itself.

Life is totally care-free, while being gently, effortlessly alive.

This is why Life, as it presently is, could be called "happy."

This is the real, only You.

* * * * *

Happiness is not something one has to *do*.

Just sit quietly and let Life's light, buoyant aliveness "come to the surface."

Feel again that Life's light, happy aliveness never shuts off.

Feel how Life simply never can *escape* being its light aliveness.

This kind of happiness is not a human emotion of happiness, which always has an opposite of sadness.

Life's natural, light happiness never is the *result* of any circumstance.

Life's light aliveness never is happy because of some situation.

It doesn't depend on any condition or any thing besides its natural light, free, aliveness to be happy.

Life can't help itself!

Life's light aliveness and ease is self-sustained and *infinite* in supply.

It's on auto-pilot.

This is *real* happiness because it can't be taken away.

* * * * *

17 Alive As Unlimited-ness

In an earlier noticing, the body was sitting quietly in the room.

The body's attention was focused on one specific item, this book.

Meanwhile, Life's un-focused awareness continued to include all items in the room and the room itself.

The *body's* focusing did not alter Life's capacity to be present and embrace even what appears as the entire universe.

Use this example again right now.

For a moment, put attention on the period at the end of this sentence.

This is the focused, limited activity of the body, or the *personal* sense of "I."

Meanwhile, the capacity to be alive, aware, and also include the entire room hasn't gone away.

This is the unlimited presence of *Impersonal* or Infinite Life.

* * * * *

Notice that the focusing of attention is capable of being *directed* from one single item to another.

That makes it limiting or finite.

Notice again how Life's all-inclusive awareness cannot be directed or focused.

It cannot be limited.

It is infinite.

As Life is infinite, it means infinity is not just a dry mathematical concept.

Infinity is *alive, aware.*

* * * * *

Notice that the focusing activity of the body or personal I is just that—*activity.*

It could be the focusing of the senses—a particular sight, a particular feeling—such as the feel of this book in the fingers.

It could be the arising of a thought or an emotion—and focusing on that.

It is as if attention goes to one small part of all experience—and that part is isolated or separated from the rest.

It's similar to focusing on a thumbnail, to the exclusion of everything else.

There is nothing wrong with focusing—it's often essential in daily living.

Nor is there anything wrong with what is focused on.

This is only pointing out that focusing is where limitations and the finite seem to be found.

* * * * *

Another thing to notice about this focused activity of the body or personal I is that it always seems to *move*.

Usually the movement is like a chain reaction.

One sensation, thought or emotion is linked to another and another throughout the day.

To focus on one thing, then the next, and the next, involves effort, energy of the body or personal I—as attention goes to each thought, feeling or sensation.

Now notice an important difference.

Feel the contrast between that *energy movement* with its constant flitting of attention—and the simple, free, effortless *present-ness* of all-embracing Life.

Like clear glass, Life's awareness always is simply present and all-embracing.

It doesn't focus, separate, react, or see in parts.

There is *no effort* because there is no focusing on any one part or single thing.

There is *no movement* from one thing to another thing.

As Life's awareness, You are still, at ease.

* * * * *

Notice what else seems to happen when focusing only on one specific item.

Suppose only this page is noticed or experienced, instead of an entire room.

When the focused attention has zeroed in on that one small part of the whole view, it's as if that part has been mentally divided from the rest.

Suddenly, that one part is treated as *separate.*

It's the same when focusing on a body and calling it "me."

Notice that a clear glass windshield cannot do that.

It always sees or includes the entire view, without separating or dividing.

Life's natural clear awareness doesn't see separate parts or divide either.

Always, Life itself is the whole.

* * * * *

That simple difference of *focusing* is the difference between being the whole of Life—or just a small part.

The very act of thinking and focusing seems to mentally create a separate "you" that is superimposed on Life's clear, whole, limitless awareness.

And this thinking seems to be something separate from Life.

This literally is the difference between *being all of Life*—or taking on an assumption of being only one small *part* of Life.

Notice that Life's awareness itself never *actually* fails to be unlimited, free Life—even if some assumptions seem to be temporarily superimposed.

It's the way the blue sky never fails to be blue even though some clouds seem to be temporarily superimposed.

* * * * *

Notice that this un-focused ease of Life's awareness is not *seeking* anything.

It is not even seeking more of itself, or a higher state of consciousness!

Life already is "at" itself.

Notice that *thinking* is what always seems to be seeking, trying to get or attain.

Thinking, by its very nature of constant movement, never is at ease.

Notice the difference when the identification is different.

If there is identification with thoughts, and an assumption that the thoughts are "you"—then "you" always are in movement, always seeking, always not at ease.

As Life's open, calm awareness—You are all the presence there is.

As Life's unlimited awareness, all is already within You.

There is nothing to seek.

* * * * *

It has been said many times that the world and all experience appears to be *within* Life's awareness, *within* Love's aliveness.

Yet Life's awareness has no physical limits—no form or shape, no borders. It is not like a physical container. So it cannot honestly be said to have an inside or an outside.

In this sense, the term *within* now is seen to be inadequate.

Expressions such as *within* have been used as a device. They only are a means of indicating there is no physical, solid world "out there" that is separate from Life, Love.

Other examples also have been used—such as a clear glass windshield, a glass ball, and a movie screen.

Their purpose has been to help expose illusion and false beliefs—and help point out the unlimited-ness that Life is.

Once the unlimited-ness of Life is clear, then all such notions of within and outside, and all concepts, can be dropped.

The concepts are useful up to a point, but become unnecessary—because Life's aliveness is unlimited regardless.

Letting go of such concepts is like letting go of the booster stage that lifts a rocket off of "earth." The booster seemed necessary at first, but if it isn't eventually released, it becomes a hindrance.

So it is with attaching to concepts—because they only limit. Life does not depend on concepts to be the unlimited Life it is.

* * * * *

Imagine a wide open, endless clear blue sky.

The sky is like Life's clear, open perceiving—uncluttered by clouds of thoughts.

Now suppose a small cloud appears.

Say this cloud is what seems to be "your" thinking.

Would any amount of *additional thinking* done by the cloud ever make things more clear and blue, like the sky?

Any additional thinking only would be *adding* to the cloudiness!

Meanwhile, the blue sky itself never is affected.

Again, the clouds just seem to be something temporarily superimposed—and never really alter the sky's blue-ness.

The sky itself is *effortlessly* and unfailingly clear blue.

It never is trying to become un-cloudy.

The way to experience clarity is not by *thinking* about Life—but by *being alive* as Life.

* * * * *

Notice all of what appears as daily experience in a new way.

Thanks to awareness, this experience now can be seen as just so much dream-like *thought*—not a separate, weighty, physical world.

But even when seen as mere thought—even that thought is limited.

It still consists of noticeable, observable, finite perceptions or mental forms—whether a "banana," or the thought of a white cat.

To be alive as Life's pure aliveness is to be alive as unlimited-ness, alive as the Infinite, and perceiving as a state of harmony.

This infinite alive presence, this unlimited-ness, is "the juice" mentioned in the Introduction.

Life's unlimited aliveness never is consciously clinging or mentally locking on to any one limiting pattern of thought.

This non-clinging or un-attached-ness of Life's pure aliveness is like a letting go. Life's ever-fresh aliveness is not stuck to anything.

When alive as this, there is freedom.

Because there is no clinging, no stuck-ness, this is what allows old thought forms or living patterns to be released and shift.

They can appear to change to *new*, more harmonious forms of thought.

The harmony is because things no longer are being mis-seen through a super-imposed filter of illusion and false beliefs.

This is why *daily experience* and even *world experience* can appear to shift and change to new, more harmonious forms, too.

It is because all there would be to that experience is *thought*.

Now it is clearly perceived by Life's *oneness*, or harmony itself.

* * * * *

18 Love Is *Alive*

Notice any reactions due to having seen the non-solidity of "body."

"What about my loved ones and friends?" the thought may come.

Notice again—there are no physical items in a dream. Nor are any items in a dream physically separate or distant from each other.

It's similar in daily life—as the sensory illusion is seen through.

No "body" really is a separate object. And there really is *zero physical distance* separating things—regardless of how it appears.

How close and immediate is *this*?!

It means "loved ones and friends" are now actually more intimate and closer than ever!

Despite appearances, there is only *one Life* present and functioning.

Life's awareness appears to embrace all things equally within its warm, gently alive presence—without judgment or preference.

This also is why Life could be called *Love*.

The words Life and Love are synonyms—just different word labels for this one unfailing and all-inclusive gentle aliveness.

It means Love is not a mere human emotion, stuck inside of bodies.

Love is an *alive, aware presence*.

Love is *this* very awareness, wherein all of existence appears to be experienced.

Love is the *invisible alive liquid* in which all existing goes on.

* * * * *

It appears as if *all* "bodies" are like thought-images within this *one* perceiving Life, Love.

So it always is this exact, same *one* Love that embraces what appears as both "your body" and "their bodies."

This one Love is an invisible alive presence—it does not have eyes. So Love does not see *visibly* the way human bodies seem to.

As Love never sees visibly, Love never sees a visible sense-illusion.

It's the way the clear blue sky does not have eyes, or see visible appearances.

Because the blue sky never "sees," it doesn't see super-imposed clouds, or see anything as separate from itself.

In the same way, Life itself, Love, never sees bodies as being separate from itself, or from each other.

Only mistaken human *body-sensing* seems to experience a visible illusion of separateness.

As Life itself does not experience separateness, it cannot experience many separate *lives*.

Life only experiences or *is*, only *one* all-present aliveness, *one* Love— always whole and complete.

This also means that, to the all-perceiving Love being alive here, now, there are no such things as enemies.

Always, there is only the distance-less immediacy of this one all-perceiving, alive Love.

It appears to silently embrace all things without label or judgment—unconditionally.

This is why Life sometimes is called *unconditional Love*.

* * * * *

Notice what's going on when music is coming over a radio.

The music does not originate from within the radio.

The capacity to write music is not inherent in the radio.

The music is from a signal that is "everywhere present" in the air.

The radio simply appears to give expression to the music.

Notice, however, that it is usually assumed the capacity to write books or music is inherent in people, in bodies.

Without there first being Life itself, could anything get written?

Isn't it really thanks to Life itself, Love, being alive that anything *does* get written?

So shouldn't "everywhere present" Love be given all the credit instead?

Think of the body that appeared to write this book as a radio.

The real author (and reader) is the one unlimited Love itself.

* * * * *

Notice also that this book and what it points out can't be coming to a "you" from another separate self or life "out there."

There really is no separate, physically distant object known as "author" from which this could come.

There really is no "out there," no physical space, in which separation could occur.

What this book is pointing out appears to be coming from, and all going on within, *this* present space-less Love, alive right here.

It is as if *this* very Life, Love, were talking to itself about itself.

* * * * *

Keep noticing that Love's aliveness alive here, now, is always present tense.

Really pause so this present-ness of Love is actually an *alive experience or taste*—rather than something merely *read about.*

Stop and specifically be alive as Love's aliveness which only is alive *presently.*

Keep noticing that Love's present aliveness is not visible, but is an *invisible* presence.

It is not a sensory experience which always comes and goes.

Love's all-presence does not come and go.

During the day, if it seems you are caught up in the constant movement of the body, you can pause frequently to ask:

"Am I a visible, constantly moving, illusory picture?"

"Or am I alive as Love's invisible, un-moving, ever-presence?"

* * * * *

The noticing on this page combines with the following page.

Feel the calm, the un-pressured-ness, of Life's alive openness as it simply is *being*.

Here, there is no stress—no thought of *trying*, or having to accomplish something.

Notice that Love's open aliveness is not thinkable, but is only feel-able or "alive-able."

Notice again how it is *always* alive and always "on."

Feel how there is no noticeable place where Love's *alive-ing* can be said to end or start.

Yet it always seems to *be present*.

Feel again how Love's invisible alive-ing has none of what could be called physical distance between itself and its own presence.

Never does Love's aliveness have to *travel* anywhere to get itself.

Feel again how this alive Love can't shut off its alive Love.

* * * * *

Now, with eyes closed, see some events from earlier in the day.

See the body getting out of bed. See it perhaps at the workplace.

Notice there are only wisps of dream-like images to those events— and no solid physical bodies.

There are no solid buildings or places involved.

There is no physical distance or depth involved.

All of it always appears "right here" on the screen of Love's alive perceiving.

The only real Life and presence for all of it is this invisible alive Love *You now are alive as.*

What's really here is the *alive immediacy of one Love* wherein there is no distance or physical separation.

Notice the distance-less immediacy of all these images appearing in Love's aliveness.

This is the way daily living is when the eyes are wide open, too.

Go back and forth.

Close the eyes and be alive as Love's invisible aliveness.

Then open the eyes again.

Notice Love's invisible aliveness still is present and *alive.*

It is effortless to be this ever-alive invisible Love.

It's simply a matter of not being distracted by the visible.

* * * * *

Imagine if, somehow, every body apparently on the planet were on a sightseeing hike together.

Someone shouts, "Hey, come check this out."

Everyone goes around a bend in the path.

Suddenly, right where the solid path and ground and trees had appeared to be—it's as if everything has turned into liquid.

The path, the entire ground, even the mountains, air and sky, still appear to be there, but now they are this liquid.

The former sense of things as being solid, separate objects has dissolved. All experience now is like a fluid.

The body continues walking through this liquid.

Even the body itself feels as liquid as everything else.

All the apparent forms in the liquid seem as if they are moving, coming and going—but the liquid itself isn't coming and going.

The liquid is pleasantly vitalizing. It feels light and pure, continuously fresh and new.

It is so pleasant, all concerns of the day seem washed away.

The liquid is not water.

It's alive.

It's Love.

It's You.

* * * * *

It is possible to go around that "bend in the path" and experience Life as liquid Love anywhere, anytime.

It is as simple as being alive as Love's invisible ease of aliveness.

It is impossible to *escape* being this alive Love.

Love's lightness and happiness literally is the very substance of all that exists.

Love's happiness never has to struggle to be—to be *all*.

Love's happiness never can be made to leave or go away—any more than *all* can go away.

Love and *all* are the same *one*.

* * * * *

19 The Softness Of Life

Notice that all of the preceding pages have been concerned with one thing.

It is simply noticing what is *already* true of pure Life, Love, itself.

This soft presence of Life is not dependent on personal ability.

It is how Life itself is *already* and unstoppably functioning.

Life itself is forever free, unlimited and un-threatened.

Notice there has been little concern with trying to improve a "you" as a separate personality.

Rather, this is making clear that Life itself really is the very one—the only one—being alive here, and Life needs no improving.

What seems to happen is that mistaken assumptions about a false "you" and its experience are exposed and fall away.

Nothing ever changes with Life itself and its endless freedom.

Life's ease of Love is always *fully alive as all that is*.

* * * * *

No one has ever gone to the supermarket to buy two pounds of Life's gently alive awareness.

So—what is it to feel once more that, as this present state of alive awareness, you have absolutely no weight?

This is the real You—again, a delightful, alive *lightness*.

As noticed earlier, Life's aliveness never goes away or is absent.

This is another way of saying Life's *lightness* never is absent.

If a feeling of heaviness tries to impose itself during the day, simply notice that the heaviness is not you, not yours.

Instead, be alive as Life's *lightness*.

After all, this is what You truly are.

What is it to know this delightful lightness is present all day long?

This is how Life itself is living—and Life is the only one being alive.

* * * * *

What if it really were possible to buy Life's gentle aliveness in the supermarket?

What a great product that would be.

Maybe the best selling product ever.

Wait a minute.

It's better than that right now.

Life's gentle aliveness always is totally free!

It is available in *unlimited* supply—always.

You can have all you want. Yet you never can use it up—because there is *no end* to the gentle, soft aliveness of Life, Love.

Best of all, one need not go anywhere to get Love's aliveness.

And it isn't something one *has*. It is the Life present here right now.

In fact, it is impossible to *not* be it.

* * * * *

Why the repeated emphasis on Life's lightness and softness?

It keeps this from being merely an intellectual exercise, and keeps it as the *consciously alive experience* it truly is.

Feel again how *endlessly soft* Love's gently alive presence is.

Life itself never is hard.

It sometimes may seem human daily experience is hard, but that's not the one Life, Love, itself.

This is a key distinction to notice.

Life is this exquisitely soft, alive ease which simply never fails to be.

It is possible to "plumb the depths" of Love's alive softness and its unfailing ease forever, and never deplete it.

In what might pass as a thousand years, it always is as fresh and new as it is *now.*

That's because Love's aliveness is not affected by time, not material or subject to change or decay.

It is eternal.

It is eternity itself.

* * * * *

Love's pure aliveness is not the same as how a body feels, which always seems grounded.

If anything, Love's light, soft aliveness is a feeling of not being grounded or attached to anything.

This un-grounded or un-attached presence may feel like it is *free*, and softly *floating*, as noticed before.

Be alive as this freedom of Love's soft, floating presence.

It feels as if there are no handles, no place to rest *on*.

Life's soft, all-embracing presence is all the presence there is—so there is nothing in addition to Life itself that Life *could* rest on!

Instead of identifying yourself as a weighty body that seems to be grounded—what is it to live Life as a softly floating presence?

Notice if there are any thoughts or judgments about this.

Does it feel uncomfortable—or just different, new?

* * * * *

When the false beliefs about earth were exposed, it was seen to be a tiny sphere, *floating* in a much larger universe of space.

That's the point—earth, too, suddenly was seen to be just floating.

In that era, imagine how a floating view must have felt quite different and new, too.

In ending that old geo-centric belief, notice a similarity to today.

To assume Life is grounded inside of bodies would be *body-centric*.

Rather than feeling centered in a grounded body, what is it to be un-grounded, free, and totally without a form—yet distinctly alive—as all the presence there is?"

What is it to really notice that no "place" can confine you as this alive presence?

Notice what it is to *never* come to an end of the ease and softness of aliveness which you are presently alive to being.

Might as well get used to this, because it is your eternal "address."

* * * *

The softness of Life's presence and experience of floating at first may *seem* unusual.

It would be only because an earlier sense of grounded-ness is gone.

Notice some things.

First—it was just a *sense* of being grounded. There is no earth-object on which Life could be grounded, so it wasn't real anyway.

Now notice closely if there is any feeling of hesitation or fear about floating. Such feelings might be due to a possibility of instability or falling.

Yet this presence of Life, Love, as it is being all-embracingly alive, is the entirety of what exists, or *all*.

The fact that Love is *all* means falling is not an option.

As Love's presence is *all, endless*, there is nowhere besides Love's own allness that Love could fall to.

As Love's softly alive allness, You are infallible.

Notice if there's a thought, "No, this can't be all. Surely there is something beyond."

Notice that the "something beyond" *always* would be just another thought—just imaginary.

And that thought always appears to arise here, within the allness that Love's awareness is.

Love never comes to an end of its allness, for Love has no end.

If *this* isn't "stable" nothing is.

* * * * *

Did you ever notice *the entire universe* is not resting on anything?

The entire universe, too, appears to be just *floating*.

You have to totally drop any notion of it being *on* something.

The universe appears to float as its own endlessness.

Pause reading a moment to really let this in.

You have to let it in.

That's because there is only one place the entire floating universe appears to be found.

Within You!

The only reason the "universe" appears to be floating is because *You* are floating!

The "universe" is just a lot of distance-less sense perceptions that appear within Love's boundless aliveness as it is here and now softly alive.

To the five senses, it may *appear* the universe is vast and spans trillions of light-years.

Yet even light-years and vast space still would be measurable and have limits.

And the universe, in all its apparent grandeur, now is seen to be mere wisps of dream-like thought.

That is just a drop in the bucket compared to You, Life's un-restrainable infinite Love.

* * * * *

This book is meant to be only a door opener.

It gets you into the party.

But the party is just beginning.

Life is always freshly alive and new—as if just beginning.

This book is at its close, yes—but notice if there is a feeling that is different from finishing other books.

Even though these pages have ended, there may be a feeling that things are unfinished, still open.

It doesn't feel as if a conclusion has been reached.

That's exactly it.

Love never does come to a conclusion because it doesn't have one.

* * * * *

Keep Noticing

For more information about the work of Peter, including workshops, webinars, books, audios and videos, and free products, please visit http://SimplyNotice.com

To contact Peter for a retreat, or a speaking engagement at your workplace or university, please use the Contact page at http://SimplyNotice.com

* * * * *

About The Author

Peter Francis Dziuban (pronounced Joobin) writes and speaks on awareness and spirituality. His first book, *Consciousness Is All*, has helped thousands around the world enjoy greater clarity, happiness, and freedom.

Peter's work benefits so many because it is not tied to any teaching or religion. He has studied this field over 40 years, since attending the University of Notre Dame. He also worked many years in corporate America. Now residing in Arizona, Peter enjoys the outdoors.

For more information, please visit: http://SimplyNotice.com

* * * * *

THE PRINCIPLES OF DESIGN

OXFORD SERIES ON ADVANCED MANUFACTURING

SERIES EDITORS

J. R. CROOKALL
MILTON C. SHAW

1. William T. Harris. *Chemical Milling: The Technology of Cutting Materials by Etching* (1976)
2. Bernard Crossland. *Explosive Welding of Metals and its Applications* (1982)
3. Milton C. Shaw. *Metal Cutting Principles* (1984)
4. Shiro Kobayashi, Soo-Ik Oh, Taylan Altan. *Metal Forming and the Finite-Element Method* (1989)
5. E. Taniguchi. *Energy Beam Processing of Materials* (1989)
6. Nam P. Suh. *The Principles of Design* (1990)

THE PRINCIPLES
OF DESIGN

NAM P. SUH

Massachusetts Institute of Technology

New York   Oxford
OXFORD UNIVERSITY PRESS
1990

Oxford University Press

Oxford   New York   Toronto
Delhi   Bombay   Calcutta   Madras   Karachi
Petaling Jaya   Singapore   Hong Kong   Tokyo
Nairobi   Dar es Salaam   Cape Town
Melbourne   Auckland

and associated companies in
Berlin   Ibadan

Library of Congress Cataloging-in-Publication Data

Suh, Nam P., 1936–
The principles of design/Nam P. Suh.
p.   cm.—(Oxford series on advanced manufacturing; 6)
Includes bibliographies and index.
ISBN 0-19-504345-6
1. Engineering design.   I. Title.   II. Series
TA174.S89   1990
620′.00425—dc19   88-19584 CIP

11   13   15   17   19   18   16   14   12

Printed in the United States of America
on acid-free paper

PREFACE

Among intellectual and technological pursuits, design is one of the oldest endeavors. From prehistoric periods, humanity has designed and made hunting implements, shelters, and clothing. It might have preceded the development of natural sciences by scores of centuries. Yet, to this day, design is being done intuitively as an art. It is one of the few technical areas where experience is more important than formal education. If the goal of education is to transmit systematic and generalizable knowledge, rather than experience, to those uninitiated in the art and science, design has not yet made the grade as an intellectual discipline, for few schools teach the subject with systematically generalizable knowledge. The ad hoc approach to design and design education has been the norm rather than the exception. Design is clearly one of the remaining intellectual challenges of the twentieth century, and perhaps beyond.

Engineering and design are almost synonymous. Engineers design. They design structures, products, software, manufacturing processes, systems, and even organizations. The decisions that they make during the design stage profoundly affect all those that follow—be it quality of the product, the durability of ancient buildings (some of which still stand today), or the quality of life. Engineers have done amazing things throughout history, but in some cases, the ad hoc decision-making process has not been as effective as it should have been. We see many failures of design, some spectacular and many routine.

There is a general consensus today that engineering schools must do a better job in teaching design, and must elevate the importance of design in our curricula. The critical issue is not whether we should teach design in our engineering schools, but rather what to teach and how to teach it.

This book presents the principles of design and constitutes a treatise or exposition of the design axioms and their applications; these axioms are the basic principles of design. This view of design has been advocated by the author during the past 10 years. This book presents work done by him and his associates, in a coherent manner, so that others may follow the thoughts behind the design axioms more systematically. This book is intended for both students and professionals.

This book was used to teach students in a graduate level course at MIT for the first time in the academic year 1987–1988. It is intended to be for a

one-semester subject and should be suitable for both undergraduate and graduate students, although some case studies may require backgrounds in advanced engineering subjects. The problems given at the end of most chapters are exercise problems that may be used as homework questions. Some of these problems do not have a single correct answer—they may have many acceptable solutions. In some cases the student is expected to define the problem through library research, or even by performing simple critical experiments.

The important thing for the student to learn is that the ability to define the problem is the most important and difficult task in engineering. We sometimes teach the student how to find solutions to "nonproblems" that are amenable to mathematical treatment using well-established techniques, rather than imparting to them the ability to solve the real problem. Case studies are extensively presented in Chapters 6–9 to illustrate the significance as well as the use of the axioms in solving real problems.

Most of this book was written while the author served in the U.S. Government as assistant director for engineering of the National Science Foundation (NSF), especially during the last 6 months of his tenure; this unexpected call to duty from the White House delayed this project by 2 years; however, the motivation to write was reinforced by the opportunity that he had at NSF.

Although NSF has tried to strengthen the design field, the community has had problems in defining research agenda and goals, especially the intellectual and scientific elements of the design field. Often many educators and engineers try to use computers to deal with design subjects, rather than to comprehend the conceptual aspect of the design process. This field will never develop the requisite intellectual base if we abdicate our power to reason and conceptualize basic principles to the computational power of machines.

Just as there are many design solutions, there must be many diverse approaches to "design science." The axiomatic approach may be one of many possible avenues toward this goal. It is the hope of the author that the axiomatic approach at least illustrates how design can be made into a science. A few years or decades from now, the contents of this book may be surpassed by more-advanced approaches, and be viewed as elementary. If this book can serve as a stepping stone in this historic development, it will have served a useful purpose.

Cambridge, Mass.   N. P. S.
April 1989

ACKNOWLEDGMENTS

During the past decade, many students and colleagues made the research on the axiomatic approach to design exciting and rewarding. They have contributed through their critical comments, their generation of important ideas and methodologies, and even through their initial skepticism about the whole notion of developing axioms for design. The author benefited a great deal through his association with them. To each one, he is deeply grateful.

Since their contributions are extensively cited throughout the book, the author will delete the specifics from this acknowledgment. However, it is his wish to mention several people whose names were very closely associated with the axiomatic research at MIT. His special thanks go to his former graduate students and partners in learning. Professors Steven H. Kim and James R. Rinderle have not only made significant contributions from the early days of its development, but have also contributed to this book by carefully reading the manuscript and/or helping to clarify some of the materials presented in this book. Messrs. K. Kaneshige, Jack Smith, William Tice, Turker Oktay, and M. Yasuhara, Dr. David Wilson, and Dr. Susan Finger also deserve special thanks for their intellectual curiosity and contributions.

Professors Adam C. Bell, Nathan H. Cook, and David Gossard, the author's colleagues at MIT who undertook the research project together with the author, made invaluable contributions to the subject matter. The scholarly discussions yielded many dividends. The author will cherish, with fondness, the sense of commitment and dedication to the task of making design and manufacturing into academic disciplines. We enlightened each other through rigorous discussions, an experience that the author was privileged to share.

The research on design has benefited a great deal from the short-term visitors to MIT, especially Professor C.M. Lee of Seoul National University, Professor H. Nakazawa of Waseda University, and Professor G. Sohlenius of The Royal Institute of Technology in Stockholm. They brought new insights to the project and made unique contributions to the design axioms and their applications.

The research work that has become the basis of this book was made possible by the financial support provided by the National Science

Foundation (NSF), numerous industrial firms, and Lawrence Livermore National Laboratory. The author is indebted to Dr Bernard Chern and Dr. John Holtzrichter.

Much of the book was written while the author was with the NSF, heading up its Engineering Directorate. The author had a chance to broaden his views on various technical, human, national, and international issues. His public service at NSF was most rewarding, thanks to the exceptionally gifted and able people who made NSF a haven for those committed to excellence. His official thanks go to his colleagues and staff in the Engineering Directorate, whose dedication to excellence and public service is without peer. The author is specially grateful to Dr. Erich Bloch, Director of NSF, who made the NSF an agent for change. Finally, life at NSF would have been less enjoyable without the friendship of many of his colleagues in the Executive Council.

His public service in the U.S. Government was made possible by the extended leave of absence granted to him by MIT. What had started out as a 1-year stint eventually became a commitment that lasted for 3 years and 3 months. This would not have been possible without the understanding support of his MIT colleagues. Dr. Paul E. Gray, Dean Gerald L. Wilson, and Professor David N. Wormley deserve his special thanks for their encouragement and appreciation for public service.

A number of colleagues throughout the world have reviewed the manuscript and made valuable comments. His appreciation goes to all of these colleagues; in particular, to Professor J. Peters of Katholieke Universiteit Leuven, Professor Milton C. Shaw of Arizona State University, and Dr. Carl W. Hall of the National Science Foundation.

The author owes a great deal to Mr. Robert G.H. McCausland, Ms. Renee Balog, Ms. Christina Ware, Ms. Margaret Herbig, and Ms. Rose Szwast for their support and assistance in preparing the manuscript. They made it fun to be involved in such an endless task.

Finally, the ideas presented in this book would not have been conceived and nurtured without the constant love and understanding the author derived from his wife and four daughters, for which he is most grateful.

TO

Young Ja

CONTENTS

THE PRINCIPLES OF DESIGN

1
INTRODUCTION

1.1 Purpose of the Book

The mid-1980s has been notable in terms of prominent engineering design failures. The Union Carbide chemical plant failure in Bhopal, India, killed more than 2,000 people; nuclear power plant accident in Chernobyl, Soviet Union, has showered many European nations with radioactive elements; the failure of an O-ring on the NASA Space Shuttle rocket booster not only killed seven brave souls but has also demoralized an entire nation; and the Three Mile Island Nuclear Power Plant accident, although of minor scope compared with the other accidents, realized the worst fears of nuclear power opponents.

Poor design practice also results in high cost and long delivery times, which may be as devastating to a firm or nation as the failure of products and structures such as those cited. It has been rumored that the U.S. Army needs 17 years to develop and field a major new weapon (such as a tank). When we recall that the Second World War lasted for only 4 years for most participants, most people would agree that 17 years is a long time. Many things can change in 17 years; the weapon may be superseded by better devices, or may even be made irrelevant by changes in political or military strategy.

There may be many reasons for such a long development process, including many nontechnical factors such as cumbersome procurement procedures. However, part of the problem may stem from technical factors: continuing alteration for functional requirements (FRs) for the weapon; incorrect or excessive FRs; wrong design decisions; and the inability to recognize faulty decisions early without having to make and test the complete prototypes.

In addition to these devastating design/manufacturing failures, many smaller problems that we encounter with our cars and home appliances may be attributed to inadequate design. Poorly designed products often cost more because they use more materials or parts than do well-designed products. (The cost of major capital equipment is nearly proportional to their weight.) They are often difficult to manufacture and to maintain. Many failures could not have been completely anticipated since products and systems are often used outside the original design "envelope"; some,

3

however, might have been averted had we a more rational approach to design than the current dependence on trial and error, intuition, empiricism, and the so-called handbook method. What is needed is a firm scientific basis for design, which can provide designers with the benefit of scientific tools that can assure them complete success.

Major design failures are easy to recognize and are often the target of inquiry by politicians, managers, and the public press. However, the design failures committed by managers and politicians are often more disastrous than engineering mistakes, although they do not often have precipitous consequences, and there are no obvious "villains."

When major corporations lose business to Japanese firms, it may be due to mismanagement, which results in undefined goals or FRs, inappropriate organizational structure, and an incorrect feedback loop, all of which might guide the corporate enterprise in the wrong direction. This means they have not correctly *designed* their organizations and/or projects. Similarly, mismanagement may be the root of the problem when a nation or city loses its entire economic base.

To have no definite goals or FRs established for the organization and/or its mission is to commit a design error. Clearly, one of the major problems in the political domain is that there are many factions or groups pulling society in many different directions, therefore making it difficult to *design* tasks, organizations, and approaches. It takes a skilled politician to prioritize goals and engineer an agenda despite the obvious conflicts.

We live in a multidimensional world. Both in the physical and in the organizational world, design must be optimized with respect to a large number of different variables. The best product must be selected from among many alternatives available, considering such diverse factors as value added, cost, accuracy, delivery time, and consumer preference. Organizations must be optimized with respect to efficiency, cost, employer morale, response time, and innovative culture. Although the design of product and organizations must often be done in a multidimensional world, managers and engineers are often taught optimization techniques for a one-dimensional world. They do not know how to think in several dimensions because they have not been given the tools and techniques that can deal with the problems of the complex world.

Everything we do in design has a *hierarchical* nature to it. That is, decisions must be made in order of importance by decomposing the problem into a hierarchy. If we want to develop a national policy to strengthen international competitiveness, the first-level decision should involve only whether or not such a national program is desirable. Only then should other decisions (such as whether a government agency or a private organization should carry out the task) be made. Once the decision on public versus private is made, the question of which agency or which private entity should execute the program should be discussed.

When such a hierarchical nature of decision making is not utilized, the process of decision making becomes very complex. A similar analogy exists

in the product development and organizational design of a firm. Proficient use of the hierarchy is a prerequisite for design or organizational success.

In order to obtain better performance, both engineering and management structures require fundamental, correct principles and methodologies to guide *decision making in design*; otherwise, the ad hoc nature of design activities cannot be improved. One of the major causes for the dismal state of design is simply mental block: the notion that design, unlike the natural sciences, cannot stand on a scientific basis. This basic hypothesis is both unnecessary and incorrect.

In the field of science, significant efforts have been made during the past several centuries to understand the "natural" processes; these endeavors have resulted in the formulation of natural laws and principles, as well as in monumental discoveries concerning the structure of life itself. Comparable efforts have *not* been made to understand the creative process involving design, synthesis, and decision-making processes. Due either to lack of sufficient effort or to the lack of truly successful paradigms for dealing with creative processes on a systematic and scientific basis based on "principles" and "laws," it has been assumed that these topics cannot be treated as subjects of scientific discourse (Simon, 1969).

However, the fact that there are *good design solutions* and *unacceptable design solutions* indicates that there exist *features* or *attributes* that distinguish between good and bad designs. Furthermore, since this creative process permeates all fields of human endeavor ranging from engineering to management, the *features* associated with good design may have *common elements*. These *common elements* may then form the basis for developing a unified theory for the synthesis process. The purpose of this book is to present such a scientific approach to design and synthesis. It presents basic elements of the process, and discusses an axiomatic approach to design and synthesis.

1.2 Introduction to Design in Engineering

Design, as the epitome of the goal of engineering, facilitates the creation of new products, processes, software, systems, and organizations through which engineering contributes to society by satisfying its needs and aspirations. Every field of engineering involves and depends on the design or synthesis process, which allows us to fulfill needs through the creation of physical and/or informational structures, including machines, software, and organizations. What is common, for example, between the design of a mechanical product and the design of governmental organization? The perceived goals of both are satisfied by an entity that provides the desired output, given a set of specified inputs; just as we cannot use an automobile to fly, so an organizational structure created to meet the needs of an engineering school cannot be used to meet the nations's long-term science and technology needs due to their disparate goals (or outputs).

Design is important because it determines the ultimate outcome of engineering activities, including the manufacturing of goods, improvement in the quality of life, and the provision of defense needs. Design decisions made at the initial or upstream stage of engineering affect all subsequent outcomes. Fine-tuning of the later stages of engineering operations may often have marginal effects on the total outcome, and certainly cannot rectify the erroneous decisions made at conception; yet we often relegate the design decisions to the least experienced or the least educated of engineering professionals. The reason why this practice has lasted for so long lies in our inability to reduce design to absolute or scientific principles, rendering the educated and uneducated alike handicapped in this field.

In the absence of a scientific basis, human intellectual endeavors ranging from fine arts to engineering are performed subjectively in the realm of the "creative" activity. Since the output of such activities cannot be understood rationally in the absence of commonly accepted criteria, they are treated as such. What this really means is that we can appreciate the outcome of the intellectual endeavor but do not understand the *process that produces the outcome,* and cannot quantify the results.

This has indeed been the case in all fields of engineering design. For example, in teaching mechanical design to students, many professors have not taught any design principles to the student in the past, but rather have acted as coaches, teaching the student ad hoc or specific techniques and boosting his or her morale. Similarly, notwithstanding its name, computer science is still largely an empirical subject lacking fundamental principles, because there is a limited amount of scientific knowledge that can be generalized and used as a guide during the synthesis processes that forms the bulk of computer science work. The immense labor required in writing software can be attributed directly to the lack of scientific principles.

Design involves *four distinct aspects* of engineering and scientific endeavor: the *problem definition* from a "fuzzy" array of facts and myths into a coherent statement of the question; the *creative process* of devising a proposed physical embodiment of solutions; the *analytical process* of determining whether the proposed solution is correct or rational; and the *ultimate check* of the fidelity of the design product to the original perceived needs.

As the adage states, "If we know what the problem is, we can find a solution"; *problem definition* is one of the most important steps in design. Problem definition is often done through an iterative process involving the complete cycle of design, which is discussed further in Chapter 2. Following the problem definition, the design process must move into the creative process. The creative process cannot be very effective without the analytical tools to judge the quality of the process itself. These two activities are as distinct as the way in which the physics of the nucleation of a bubble differs from the physics of its growth.

It is sometimes difficult to judge whether or not the problem definition

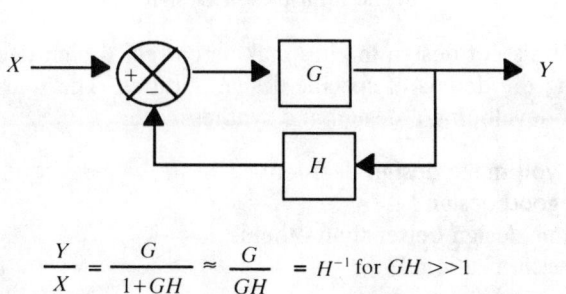

$$\frac{Y}{X} = \frac{G}{1+GH} \approx \frac{G}{GH} = H^{-1} \text{ for } GH \gg 1$$

Figure 1.1. Feedback control loop depicting the design process. Y is the desired output, X is the input, G is the synthesis capability, and H is the analytical ability. Large GH helps the sign process. The ability to judge the quality of the design quickly helps the design process.

does correctly represent the perceived needs until the final output of the design process in the form of products, processes, or systems is compared with the perceived needs. We need to improve the problem definition when the solution does not satisfy the need. The more knowledge the designer possesses through experience and/or education, the greater is the probability that the problem definition is correct. Since the problem definition is subjective, different designers may end up defining a different set of design requirements for the same perceived needs (or design problems). This is one of the reasons why there can be an infinite number of different design solutions.

The second step of the design process is the creative process of synthesizing a design solution in the form of physical embodiment. This is an *ideation* process, which is highly subjective. The creative ideas and the synthesis process depend on the specific knowledge possessed by the designer, and on his or her ability to integrate knowledge. If we give the same set of FRs for the design of a product to 10 designers, we may come up with at least 10 different ideas for the product. This issue is discussed further in Section 1.3.

The creative process in design is complemented by the analytical process. This aspect is illustrated in Fig. 1.1, which depicts the design process as a feedback control loop. It shows how the creative process must be checked through analysis and corrected for differences between the perceived problem definition and the proposed solution. In the figure, Y is the desired outcome and X the input. The gain of the feedback loop should be as large as possible to converge to a correct solution quickly; that is, the ability to judge the quality of the outcome of the creative process improves the creative process itself. In the figure, the former is depicted by the function H and the latter by G. When $G \times H$ is much larger than unity, the gain is equal to $1/H$. If we cannot analyze a design solution, then we cannot rapidly generate the "best" design since we cannot distinguish a good design from a bad design. In the absence of a criterion for selecting a good design, we cannot make good *design decisions*.

The "analysis" of design implies making correct design decisions as well as evaluating the details of specific design features. The questions that we must ask in developing a design and synthesis are:

1. How do you make design decisions?
2. Is this a good design?
3. Why is this design better than others?
4. Is my decision rational?
5. Can it be made?
6. Shall I make this in one piece or two pieces? Why?
7. How many design parameters (DPs) do I need to satisfy the FRs?
8. Shall I abandon this idea or simply modify it?
9. I thought that was a good idea. Why didn't it work?

To implement these questions, consider the design of a refrigerator door. The first decision that we have to make is what FRs the door has to satisfy. Suppose we decided there are two FRs: to provide an insulated enclosure to minimize energy loss and to provide access to the food in the refrigerator. Given these two FRs, what kind of door would you design? If someone proposed a vertically hung door (Fig. 1.2) that can be opened horizontally, like most commercial refrigerator doors, would you agree that it is a good design? If not, why do you think it is not a good design? These questions cannot be answered definitively in the absence of principles or axioms.

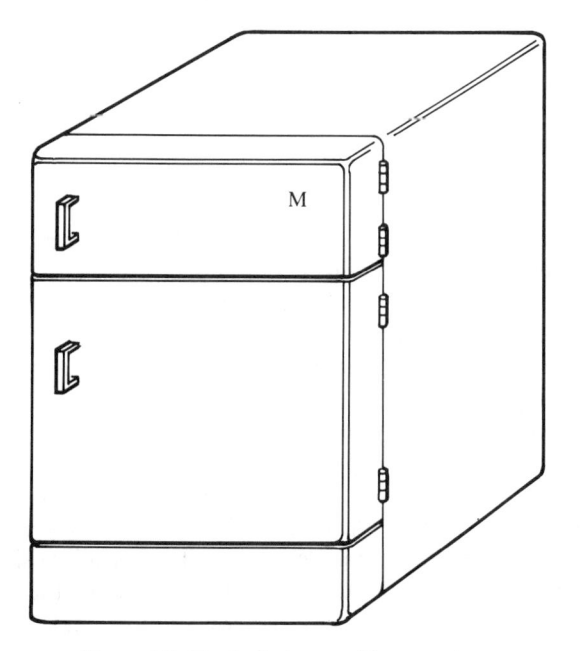

Figure 1.2. Vertically hung refrigerator door.

The design axioms that this book discuss provide principles that can answer these questions, and thus aid the creative process of design by enabling good designs to be identified from an infinite number of plausible designs. It should again be noted that all design decisions, whether they are for products, processes, systems, software, or organizations, involve the same principles.

The design axioms are conceptually simple. There are only two axioms: the *Independence Axiom and the Information Axiom.* They may be stated in declarative form as follows (Suh, 1984; Suh et al., 1978, 1979):

> Axiom 1   *The Independence Axiom*
> Maintain the independence of functional requirements (FRs).
>
> Axiom 2   *The Information Axiom*
> Minimize the information content.

The meaning of these two axioms is explored fully in the remainder of this book. In order to use these axioms, we must be familiar with the definitions of key words and terms. For the time being, it suffices to say that, according to Axiom 1, the vertically hung door is *not* a good design: the two FRs of the door (namely insulation and access) cannot be independently satisfied, since energy is lost when the door is opened to procure food. In other words, the two FRs are coupled. What, then would be a better design for the refrigerator door?

1.3 On Creative Activity and Current Design Practice

As stated earlier, once the problem is defined, design consists of two distinct processes: the *creative process,* where new ideas or solutions are synthesized in the absence of prior examples, and the *analytical process,* where design decisions must be made by evaluating the new ideas proposed. The creative process depends strongly on the designer's knowledge base and creativity, and is subjective. Therefore, there can be an infinite number of possible creative solutions that can be synthesized to satisfy the same set of requirements. However, the analytical process is deterministic, and is based on a finite set of basic principles. These two processes are interrelated, since one must be able to abandon or discard bad ideas quickly to enable the designer to create other new ideas by exploring different possibilities.

In this sense, the design axioms, which are the basic principles for analysis and decision making, help the creative process of the design activity. In the absence of basic principles or axioms, the analytical process was inoperative, and design has therefore been treated as a mysterious creative process, rather than as a rational and systematic activity. Many researchers on design concentrated on understanding the creative process of design, not having recognized the dual elements of the design process.

In the absence of principles or axioms that could be used as absolute foundations or referents, design decisions can only be made on an ad hoc or empirical basis. In this regard, design and other creative subjects such as art, have shared many common characteristics and problems. We recognize and understand special features of the fine arts, but we are unable to describe quantitatively the ultimate combination of elements that make each subject distinctive and invariant in a spatial and temporal coordinate frame. Therefore, we depend on analogy, imitation, experience, extrapolation, interpolation, and suboptimization processes to do the best we can in dealing with various tasks. Through this random process, some among us have produced truly creative breakthroughs, but they are the exceptions rather than the rule. Unfortunately, most of these geniuses could not pass the kernel of their ideas and techniques in precise statements on to younger generations. Their instinctive talents could not be captured in simple statements, for they did not understand what they knew and were unable to express their natural instincts in words.

This situation has persisted throughout the history of humanity, as intuition and experience are not absolute and objective; moreover, even "good" intuition and experience cannot be transmitted to succeeding generations in the absence of the ability to describe one's knowledge. When "know-how" and knowledge are not codified, each generation must gain similar experience all over, again and again, and develop its own intuition. These are typical characteristics of a field that has not yet matured into a "science." A truly scientific discipline is powerful because governing principles or laws describe the underlying thought process and reduce a seemingly complex array of facts and observations into consistent and explicitly stated knowledge. The ability to generalize this knowledge has accelerated the advancement of science and technology during the past two centuries. The explosion of knowledge in biological science since the discovery of DNA early in the 1950s is a case in point.

We often refer to the fine arts as a creative field. Because we do not fully understand the thought processes that lead to art, we refer to the phenomenon as *creativity* or a *creative process*. However, creativity is important in all synthesis processes, regardless of specific fields; it is simply the ability to generate new ideas or synthesize new solutions in the absence of prior examples or paradigms. Current design practice has been characterized by the creative process as defined for the fine arts. However, the field of design needs a science base, or absolute principles and axioms that can properly guide human endeavor. This is the only way to accumulate design knowledge and meet human aspirations without drawing on more-tangible resources. If we have to treat every bit of knowledge as an isolated fact, and store the knowledge in its raw, ungeneralized form, the required data base will become so immense that it cannot be retained or managed, even with the most ideal information-processing system. What the design axioms do is to complement and aid the creative process by providing the analytical tool for evaluation of the synthesized ideas so as to enable the selection of only good ideas.

Much work has been done to understand the creative process and develop a *design methodology* that can systematize the design process (Asimow, 1962; Buhl, 1962; Fasal, 1965; Zwicky, 1948). Many techniques have been advanced to enhance the creative process. For example, Harrisberger (1966) lists the following techniques which can be used to aid the design process:

1. Trigger-work technique.
2. Checklist technique.
3. Morphological technique.
4. Attribute-seeking technique.
5. Gordon technique.
6. Brainstorming technique.

Many authors present *rules* for design in various situations (Glegg, 1960; Woodson, 1966) as well as general methodologies (Alger and Hayes, 1964; Hill, 1970; Ostrofsky, 1977; Starr, 1963). In addition to these, design rules that can be used during assembly have recently been developed by Boothroyd (1981, 1987). Many software packages have also been created to assist the designer, such as those for mold making (e.g., mold flow). Finally, the utility function method has been widely used as a mathematical tool for decision making.

These techniques are either algorithmic, which apply design rules or classification methods to a specific situation (e.g., Boothroyd, 1981; Buhl, 1962; Glegg, 1960; Yoshikawa, 1985), or are not generalizable. They lack fundamental principles that can be applied to all design situations. The most easily generalized among these is the morphological technique by Zwicky (1948), which concerns itself with the intrinsic structural characteristics of the formation and content of the thought process.

In essence, the morphological technique develops a matrix of important characteristic parameters on which the solution depends, and proposes various approaches to problem solving based on the explicit statement of the problem. Following this, the performance value of each potential solution is determined. However, even this technique does not tell us how to choose the best solution since it does not provide the fundamental principles that allow for the selection of good designs without laborious calculation of all parameters (Allen, 1962). The final selection of an acceptable design by the morphological method is still ad hoc.

A version of the morphological approach is shown in Figs. 1.3 and 1.4 (Pahl and Beitz, 1984; Roth, 1982). The figures illustrate the use of design catalogues as a collection of known information for a specific problem (Hubka and Eder, 1987). Figure 1.3 is a matrix of various desired functions (i.e., the first column of the figure), and various physical effects that can relate the outputs of the system to the inputs to the system. For example, it shows that if the input energy in the form of electricity is to be converted to thermal energy, then the designer has the choice of using Joule heating, Peltier-effect, electric arc, and eddy current.

Figure 1.4 shows the various manufacturing processes that may be

Function	Input	Output	Physical effects					
E_mech → E_mech	Force, pressure, torque	Length, angle	Hooke (tension/compressiory bending)	Shear torsion	Upthrust Poisson's effect	Boyle-Marione	Coulomb I and II	...
		Speed	Energy law	Conservation of linear momentum	Conservation of angular momentum	Boyle-Mariotte	...	...
		Acceleration	Newton's law	Conservation of momentum	...	...	...	...
	Length, angle	Force, pressure, torque	Coulomb I and II	...	...	...	...	...
	Speed	— — —	Hooke	Shear torsion	Gravity	Upthrust	Centrifugal force	Capillary
	Acceleration	— — —	Coriolis force	...	Magnus-effect	Energy law	Eddy current	...
E_mech → E_hyd	Force, length, speed, pressure	Speed, pressure	Bernoulli	Viscosity (Newton)	Toricelli	Gravitational pressure	Boyle-Mariotte	Conservation of momentum
E_hyd → E_mech	Speed	Force, length	Profile lift	Turbulence	Magnus-effect	Flow resistance	Back pressure	Reaction Principle
E_hyd → E_therm	Force, speed	Temperature, quantity of heat	Friction (Coulomb)	1st law	Thomson-Joule	Hysteresis (damping)	Plastic deformation	...

Figure 1.3. Design catalog of physical effects for "change energy." (From Hubka and Eder, 1987.)

Function	Input	Output	Physical effects						
$E_{therm} \rightarrow E_{mech}$	Temperature, heat	Force, pressure, length	Thermal expansion	Steam pressure	Gas law	Osmotic pressure	...		
$E_{elect} \rightarrow E_{mech}$	Voltage, current, magn. field	Force, speed, pressure	Biot-Savart effect	Electro-kinetic effect	Coulomb I	Capacitance effect	Johnsen-Rhabeck Piezoeffect	...	
$E_{mech} \rightarrow E_{elect}$	Force, length, speed, pressure	Voltage current	Induction	Electro-kinetics	Electro-dynamic effect	Piezoeffect	Frictional electricity	Capacitance effect	
$E_{elect} \rightarrow E_{therm}$	Voltage current	Temperature, heat	Joule heating	Peltier-effect	Electric arc	Eddy current	...	...	
$E_{therm} \rightarrow E_{elect}$	Temperature, heat	Voltage current	Electrical conduction	Thermoeffect	Thermionic emission	Pyroelectricity	Noise-effect	Semiconductor, superconductor	
$E_{mech} \rightarrow E_{mech}$	Force, length, pressure, speed	Force, length, pressure, speed	Lever	Wedge	Poisson's Effect	Friction	Crank	Hydraulic effect	
$E_{hyd} \rightarrow E_{hyd}$	Pressure, speed	Pressure, speed	Continuity	Bernoulli	...	...	...	...	
$E_{therm} \rightarrow E_{therm}$	Temperature, heat	Temperature, heat	Heat conduction	Convection	Radiation	Condensation	Evaporation	Freezing	
$E_{elect} \rightarrow E_{elect}$	Voltage current	Voltage current	Transformer	Valve	Transistor	Transducer	Ohm's law		

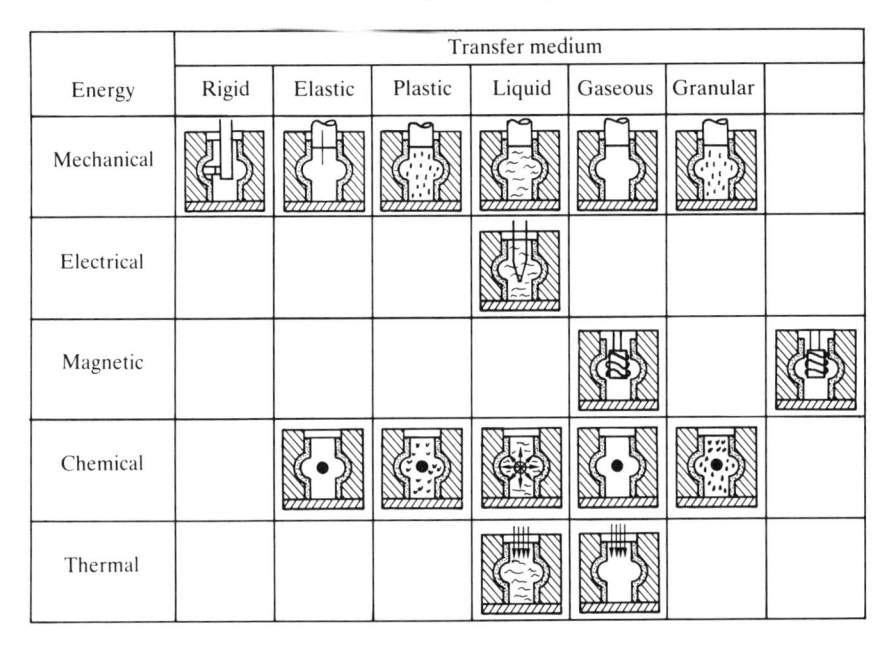

Energy	Transfer medium						
	Rigid	Elastic	Plastic	Liquid	Gaseous	Granular	
Mechanical	▦	▦	▦	▦	▦	▦	
Electrical				▦			
Magnetic				▦			▦
Chemical		▦	▦	▦	▦	▦	
Thermal				▦	▦		

Figure 1.4. Design catalog matrix for "energy transfer for forming." (From Hubka and Eder, 1987.)

designed in order to deform a cylindrical shell, using various energy sources and energy transfer media. For example, it shows that electrical energy (in the form of electric arc discharge) can be used together with liquid media to deform the shell. This representation is graphical, and perhaps more suitable as a design representation. The matrix presents all possible design options, but we must still resort to basic principles in selecting a rational design among all these possible solutions.

1.4 Axioms and the Development of Science and Technology: A Historical Perspective

In many ways the history of science and technology is closely intertwined with the development of axioms. In this sense, the development of an axiomatic approach to design is just one small step in this larger historical process. One of the earliest use of axioms was in geometry, commonly known as euclidean geometry.

Euclid (ca. 300 B.C.) developed his geometry from a set of fundamental postulates or axioms. Although the paradigm lacks the rigor of modern geometry, Euclid's *Elements* begins with definitions, postulates and axioms. Euclidean geometry was used by Newton to reduce Kepler's observations of planets to axioms describing the motion of objects and the gravitational attraction between bodies. Newton's laws were in agreement

with all observations of nature at that time, and were believed to be universal in their application. These axioms could not be proven, but were assumed to be valid as long as there were no exceptions or counterexamples. For example, Newton could not prove the relation $F = ma$, nor could he prove that action is equal to reaction. Indeed, the concept of force can only be defined in terms of his axioms; that is, we cannot measure the force directly.

In the early twentieth century, Einstein proposed a more fundamental axiom, that the speed of light is absolute, and not relative to the motion of the observer. This axiom, which led to the use of Riemann geometry and more-general forms of Newton's laws, is presently the most fundamental principle governing mechanics. Einstein's work did not invalidate the axioms of Newton, but it did clarify the domain of applicability of classical mechanics.

In many fields of science, empiricism and technological needs have always preceded the development of the science base, ranging from mathematics (von Neumann, 1961) to thermodynamics. This is best illustrated by examining the development of steam engines as a technological solution to meet a specific societal need, and the subsequent research work that led to *thermodynamics* as a scientific discipline. From the early- to mid-nineteenth century, there were many attempts to develop steam engines. In those days the axioms of thermodynamics were not established and designers therefore had to try many different ideas without the benefit of thermodynamics. Each inventor developed various "engines" by trial and error, and claimed that these engines were better than the rest. There was no way of distinguishing the advantages of one design over another without actually building the system and testing it.

This chaotic method for developing energy-conversion devices might have persisted to this day had it not been for the conceptual contributions made by Carnot and Joule during the latter part of the nineteenth century. They proposed the underlying fundamental processes involved in steam engines. These thermodynamic principles, formalized by Clausius, are the first and second laws of thermodynamics, which can now be derived from the equilibrium axiom (Hatsopoulous and Keenan, 1981).

These principles established the concept of energy and entropy in a fundamental sense, and provided the tools with which to eliminate perpetual-motion machines from consideration at the design stage. They also enable us to compute the theoretical limits and the efficiencies of proposed energy systems. These laws largely eliminated unfruitful arguments over the mertis of many energy-conversion devices through the establishment of a theoretical base.

It is interesting to note an important paradigm, based on the review of the historical development of the thermodynamic field: societal needs lead to invention and technology, and the innovations in turn create the science base as the technology is used more extensively, which in turn impacts on many other technological developments. In the case of thermodynamics, it

was the need to replace the horses that pulled ships along canals in Europe that led to the invention of steam engines. In turn, the invention of steam engines, gave the impetus to develop the science of thermodynamics. Since then, thermodynamics has had a major impact on all aspects of technology development. In this sense the science of thermodynamics was originally driven by technology. Another example of the technology-driven field that led to the science base is the communications field. The need to communicate led to the invention of telephones, which in turn led to an information theory, which has had profound impacts on many other technologies.

In contrast to these technology-driven fields, there are many science-driven fields where scientific discoveries have led to technological development. The discovery of DNA and the development of biotechnology illustrate this point. Also, the discovery of the principles for MASER and LASER led the current explosion of various optical technologies. In all cases, once the science base is established, it in turn drives the technology.

1.5 Role of Computers in Design and the Axiomatic Approach

Engineering practice and scientific inquiries are undergoing a profound change, just as the society at large has been transforming, due to the advent of computers. The ever-decreasing cost of computer hardware, and the ever-increasing computational speed and size of memory make computers a powerful tool in all segments of industialized society. Clearly, computers are having a significant impact in the design field. Graphic representation of design concepts, rapid generation of hard copies with all specific details of a design, vast data base storage and manipulation, integration of design and manufacturing, design of chemical molecules, construction of multinational service operations of all kinds, and even the design of intelligent computers, are possible because of advances in the computer field. This trend will continue well into the foreseeable future.

Various expert systems and other artificial intelligence (AI) based programs have been developed according to ad hoc design rules. These programs are used in (VLSI) circuit design, assembly (Boothroyd, 1981), and other applications. Most of these programs are rule-based interactive software programs, where the design answers are arrived at through a series of queries.

Computers cannot yet make design decisions based on their own built-in intelligence. Truly intelligent computers for design cannot be developed until the basic principles that have general applicability in all synthesis processes are incorporated as part of the computer software. Ad hoc rule-based software systems cannot provide the intelligence for computers because even the most ideal computers cannot deal with the vast data base that will be needed to anticipate all different possibilities in a general design situation.

A fundamental limitation of computer-based technology is given by Bremmerman's limit (Bremmerman, 1983). Bremmerman's argument is as follows. Suppose we make the entire Earth into the most efficient computer. The total energy, E, available for computational purpose is

$$E = mc^2 \qquad (1.1)$$

where m is the mass of the Earth and c is the speed of the light. If the total energy can be divided into ΔE increments to create a binary system for information storage, then the total bits, N, of information that we can store in the computer is

$$N = E/\Delta E \qquad (1.2)$$

In order to maximize N, we need to make ΔE as small as possible. However, Heisenberg's uncertainty principle states that the uncertainty in ΔE is related to the uncertainty in the time increment, Δt, by the relation

$$h/2\pi \le \Delta E\, \Delta t \qquad (1.3)$$

where h is Planck's constant. Equation 1.3 states that as we decrease the energy increment, Δt must be increased. Substituting Eq. 1.2 into Eq. 1.3, the total bits of information that can be handled by the "Earth computer" is

$$N \le 2\pi(E\, \Delta t/h) = 2\pi(mc^2\, \Delta t/h) \qquad (1.4)$$

If we assume that Δt is of the order of the period of atomic vibration, then the computer cannot deal with more than 270 variables at a time in a factorial design. In many design situations the total number of variables involved may be larger than 270 variables.

This is one of the many reasons why the axiomatic approach to design makes a great deal of sense. When basic principles are available for decision making in design, the number of variables and the data base required for all contingencies can be reduced significantly.

In order to be able to use the design axioms in the synthesis process, we must first understand the significance of the axioms and their implications, and then we must be able to express the axioms mathematically and develop a software language. In Chapter 10 predicate logic and PROLOG are used to establish the foundation for use of the design axioms in computers. Although much work needs to be done to develop a "user-friendly" software, an important beginning has been made.

1.6 Axiomatic Approach to Design and the Origin of the Design Axioms

The historical examples of axioms given in Sec. 1.4 deal with natural processes and the laws of nature, which differ from the synthesis process. Some may argue that there cannot be axioms in the "artificial" domain

since there (some claim) everything is *arbitrary* and *subjective*, whereas everything is *real* and *definitive* in the natural sciences. This argument is wrong in that even physical variables such as force, energy, and entropy are not primary quantities that can be measured directly, but rather are themselves products of the axioms describing nature. For example, we cannot measure force directly; we deduce it from the measurements of the dead weight of a mass, or the deflection of a spring, or the acceleration of a mass. Similarly, we deduce energy based on the first law of thermo-dynamics by measuring indirect phenomena such as the work done, the velocity of the mass, or the temperature rise.

The basic assumption of an axiomatic approach to design is that there exists a fundamental set of principles that determines good design practice. The only way to refute this assumption is to uncover counterexamples that prove these axioms to be invalid. The knowledge in a given field can be axiomatized when a set of self-consistent logic based on the axioms can yield correct solutions to all classes of problems. So far, no-one has come up with evidence that the design axioms are invalid.

The axiomatic approach to design differs philosphically from the current trend in the engineering field, which relies on large computers with vast data bases, as discussed in the preceding section. A fundamental limitation of computer-based technology given by Bremmerman's limit (Bremmer-man, 1983) makes it imperative that basic principles, and the methodol-ogies that stem from the principles, provide the conceptual framework and explicit tools for design, thus eliminating the need for an exhaustive search of all possibilities. The immense new intellectual horizon that will open up for engineering and science when intelligent computers can synthesize the optimum design solution will transform many fields, including engineering. These are some of the reasons for exploring an axiomatic approach to design and synthesis.

The questions often asked concerning axiomatic design are, "How do you generate axioms?" "How do you know they are axioms?" The simple answer is that axioms are formal statements either of what people already know, or of the knowledge imbedded in many things that people do or use routinely. Just as thermodynamic axioms (or laws) were generated based on steam engines that produced net work, design axioms are also founded upon physical observations. In order to illustrate this point, as well as to establish the cultural setting in which this kind of work is done, it may be of interest to go through a historical sketch of events leading to the design axioms.

The axiomatic approach to design and manufacturing was born out of the need to develop the disciplinary base for these fields, and to teach engineering students generalizable fundamental knowledge. The work was started in 1977, when the author was asked by Professor Herbert H. Richardson, who was then head of the mechanical engineering depart-ment, to establish a center for manufacturing research and education at MIT. The need for such a center was determined by major studies done at

MIT under the direction of the then dean of engineering, Professor Alfred Keil. The author was given $40,000 and the part-time assistance of two then-junior colleagues, Professors Adam C. Bell and David C. Gossard. In developing the long-term goals and strategic plans of the Laboratory for Manufacturing and Productivity (LMP), the author realized that a sad period in MIT's engineering education should not be repeated.

In the late-1950s and early-1960s, due to the perceived Soviet scientific advantage embodied in Sputnik, and because of the drop in engineering enrollment, engineering education was in turmoil. Many educators believed that this "demise" was due to the insufficient emphasis of *engineering science* in engineering education. In some ways it was a repetition of the historical argument over the proper course of engineering education. Ever since the 1860s, when engineering schools were established for the first time in the United States, two schools of thought have dominated engineering education: those that believed that the role of engineering education is to introduce scientific principles and methodologies into engineering practice and those that advocated the emphasis on the practice of engineering through acquisition of "hands-on" experience.

The fact of the matter is that an engineer needs both of these. In engineering, the first step toward developing a solution is the *synthesis* of the overall solution, which involves conceptualization and design of an overall solution by *integrating* empirical knowledge and scientific principles. This step is then followed by the *optimization* process, which involves the dissection of the design into components, and the analysis of each component using scientific principles and mathematical tools. That is, engineering consists of analysis *and* synthesis, science-driven *and* technology-driven fields, natural *and* artifical laws, scientific *and* technological factors, *as well as* human and societal issues. Engineering education must provide a balanced input of these diverse elements of engineering to the student.

Unfortunately, during the past three decades, the education system has treated engineering as synonymous with engineering science. Some influential people in engineering education in the early-1960s wanted to eliminate "nonscientific" engineering subjects from the curriculum, and de-emphasize research in empiricism-dominated fields such as design and manufacturing. This point of view overshadowed the thinking of all leading engineering schools in the United States. As a result, engineering education in the United States gave primary emphasis to analysis and neglected technology-driven subjects such as design; engineering became synonymous with engineering science.

What they should have done, but did not do, was to change the research emphasis of these empiricism-dominated fields in order to establish a scientific base and develop these fields into disciplines. We needed a stronger engineering science base, but not at the expense of a strong design capability and technology-driven fields.

In light of this historical precedent, the author, as director of this new

effort at MIT, decided to establish a disciplinary base for design and manufacturing through an axiomatic approach to design and manufacturing as part of the center's efforts. The rationale was the need always to deal with natural processes *and* artificial processes, and the imperatives of teaching the engineering student not only the natural laws of nature, but also the artifacts of the design world. The author is still convinced that only through the establishment of the science base can the design and manufacturing fields become a discipline.

Having reached this conclusion, the author, together with his colleagues Adam Bell and David Gossard as faculty associates, proposed to the National Science foundation (NSF) a research program on an axiomatic approach to manufacturing/design. After discussing this proposed work with the NSF program director for production engineering, Dr. Bernard Chern, a formal proposal entitled "Exploratory Study of Constraints in Design by Functional Requirements and Manufacturing" was submitted. Dr. Chern convinced us that this long title was better than "An Axiomatic Approach to Design and Manufacturing." The proposal did not state what the axioms were or how they were to be derived, but simply that we wanted to create axioms for decision making in design.

Dr. Chern decided that the best way to evaluate this "unusual" proposal was to bring a site-visiting team to MIT, since the proposed work was so "far out" that "mail-review" would not be able to deal with the subject. Two days before the site visit, the author, while at the University of West Virginia to deliver a lecture, received an urgent telephone call from Professor Gossard; he had met some of the site-visiting team members (six academics and six industrial engineers) at the University of Massachusetts at Amherst, where the North American Manufacturing Research Conference had been held. The team was wondering how we actually planned to create the axioms (although no-one objected to the overall goal of the project).

The author had 24 hours to prepare an answer to this question. After dinner at a renowned restaurant, called Burger King, near the university campus he went back to his assigned room at the West Virginia University and decided to develop a set of "hypothetical" axioms, to respond to the basic question of the reviewers. Since this proposed work was the centerpiece of the newly formed laboratory, the support for the project was crucial to the success of the laboratory. Therefore, the author prepared himself mentally for this site visit as if he was preparing for a major battle.

In order to develop the hypothetical axioms, the author considered several projects that he had worked on in industry and at universities, and that had turned out to be very successful, and tried to identify the common elements present in all. He then tried to generalize these common elements. Among his patents and projects selected for this consideration were the following: the foam/straight plastic laminating/molding process, the USM high-pressure foam molding techique, the electrically conductive

grinding wheel, the electrical ignition of double-base propellant, and coated carbide tools.

Out of this mental exercise evolved 12 "hypothetical" axioms, which were literally written on the back of an envelope. The following evening he returned to MIT and regrouped with Adam and David to discuss the 12 "hypothetical" axioms. It became apparent through the discussion that these could be reduced to six "hypothetical" axioms and six corollaries.

Having established at least a plausible method toward generating axioms, we then presented the strategy to the site-visiting team on the following morning. We concluded that I should make an overall presentation including the hypothetical axioms, that Bell should present a case study related to his area of specialization, namely *assembly*, and Gossard should likewise present a topic related to sheet metal forming. (The material we prepared for the presentation was the basis of our first paper on the topic: Suh et al., 1978).

The meeting lasted for 1 day, and we had a lively discussion; the review was positive. However, it took an additional year to receive funds. Meanwhile, four graduate students were hired to work on this project, based solely on the encouraging review of the site-visit panel. The unexpected delay in funding obviously created a great financial strain for the laboratory since graduate students were promised funding. We proceeded to work on the project, whereupon we quickly realized that the six "hypothetical" axioms could be further reduced to two axioms. Although we planned to add a few more, to this date we have not come up with any new axioms.

By 1984 LMP had become a large and successful organization with substantial industrial funding. At this early stage of its development, however, the success of each project in terms of research funding was critical. Since MIT could not finance the establishment of such a new laboratory solely from its own resources, outside funding was key to the survival of LMP.

This fund-driven university research enterprise is historically unique to the United States in this era, having had both positive and negative impacts on universities. It has created or reinforced the two-tier university system in which 20 or so research universities have created a formidable research/education system and set themselves apart from other, primarily teaching, institutions. Because of this heavy emphasis on research, innovations in teaching have not received top priority at many universities. Further-more, much of the research consisted of analysis that has been the predominant research culture of the past 30 years. Notwithstanding these shortcomings, U.S. eductation/research enterprise is strong and dynamic as it approaches the twenty-first century, because of its vital base of education and research.

One of the reasons for writing this book is to contribute to the transition from the engineering science-dominated era to the era of balanced engineering education through the establishment of academic disciplines

for design and manufacturing. Nearly every subject in engineering schools and the whole philosophy of engineering education must give a balanced emphasis to the design (or synthesis) and analysis. The student must be taught to see the big picture and the ability to conceptualize a solution, as well as how to optimize an existing product or process. The student must be involved in the exciting world of engineering where creative minds thrive, and where exact sciences temper new creation with precision for the benefit of the larger society.

1.7 Introduction to the Book

This book develops the principles of design based on the design axioms. It is a treatise on the subject matter. Since it is the first comprehensive book on the axiomatic approach to design, it does not have the benefit of learning from the mistakes that other books might have made in clarifying the basic concepts involved in using the design axioms. Therefore, some sections may not provide sufficient explanations, whereas other sections may dwell on simple concepts for too long. These are the risks that this kind of book undertakes.

Chapter 2 defines and describes design processes and design. It gives definitions of the key terms used throughout the book, and explains the hierarchical nature of FRs and DPs. It also presents the concept of the *design helix* as a means of showing the dynamic nature of the product development process.

Chapter 3 presents the *designs axioms,* their corollaries and some theorems. This chapter presents the basic concepts involved, using examples, in addition to providing the formalism required to develop the axiomatic basis of design. In the appendices for this chapter, detailed analyses of the examples discussed qualitatively in the main text show the link between synthesis and analysis.

Chapter 4 discusses the *Independence Axiom* in detail. The basic concept is illustrated graphically as well as analytically. The significance of the tolerance in measuring the functional independence is discussed. The metrics for measuring functional independence are also defined.

Chapter 5 is a counterpart to Chapter 4 in connection with the *Information Axiom*. It defines the information content in terms of probability, and describes how the information can be measured when the system capability and the designer specification for certain functions differ.

Chapter 6 is the first of four chapters dealing with applications. This chapter presents nine case studies involving the design of manufacturing processes and intelligent machines. Chapter 7 deals with case studies involving the design of products, whereas Chapter 8 includes case studies that are based solely on the Information Axiom. One of the case studies in Chapter 8 illustrates the wide applicability of the axioms; it deals with the question of which automobile is the best buy. Chapter 9 expands the

concept of design by presenting case studies involving the use of the axioms in designing organizations and manufacturing systems.

Chapter 10 demonstrates how the design axioms can be presented mathematically, and thereby utilized in software development and computer applications. Chapter 11 summarizes the key points presented in earlier chapters.

Throughout the book, problems are presented at the end of chapters. Some of these problems are brief exercise problems, whereas others are open-ended design problems that require library or laboratory work. A great deal of emphasis is placed on problem definition, which is one of the most important elements in the design process.

One of the best ways of understanding the axioms and theoretical materials is to go through the case studies. The reader should read case studies whenever appropriate, rather than reading the chapters in sequence.

1.8 Summary

This introductory chapter emphasizes the importance of an axiomatic approach to design and synthesis, in light of both the historical development of science and technology, and of the need to unify and generalize available knowledge in the design field. It also relates, as a historical note, how these axioms were developed and how research is presently conducted at our universities.

References

Alger, R.M., and Hays, C.V., *Creative Synthesis in Design*. Prentice-Hall, Englewood Cliffs, NJ, 1964.

Allen, M.S., *Morphological Creativity*. Prentice-Hall, Englewood Cliffs, NJ, 1962.

Asimow, M., *Introduction to Design*, Prentice-Hall, Englewood cliffs, NJ, 1962.

Boothroyd, G., "Design for Manufacturability," Videorecording, Center for Advanced Engineering Studies, MIT, Cambridge, MA, 1981.

Boothroyd, G., "Design for Assembly—The Key to Design for Manufacture," *The International Journal of Manufacturing Technology*, 2:3–11, 1987.

Bremmerman, H. J., "Optimization through Evolution and Recombination," *Self-Organizing Systems*. Spartan Books, Chicago, 1983.

Buhl, H. R., *Creative Engineering Design*. Iowa State University Press, Ames, IA, 1962.

Fasal, J., "Force Decisions for Value," *Product Engineering*, April 12, 1965.

Glegg, G.L., *Design of Design*. Cambridge University Press, NY, 1960.

Harrisberger, L., *Engineermanship: A Philosophy of Design*, Brooks/Cole, Belmont, CA, 1966.

Hatsopoulous, G., and Keenan, J.M., *Principles of General Thermodynamics*. Robert E. Kreiger Publ. Co. Huntington, NY, 1981.

Hill, P.H., *The Science of Engineering Design*. Holt, Rinehart and Winston, NY, 1970.

Hubka, V., and Eder, W.E., "A Scientific Approach to Engineering Design," *Design Studies* **8**(3):123–137, 1987.

Ostrofsky, B., *Design, Planning and Development Methodology*. Prentice-Hall, Englewood Cliffs, NJ, 1977.

Pahl, G., and Beitz, W., *Engineering Design*. The Design Council, London, 1984.

Roth, K., *Konstruieren mit Konstruktionsanlagen*. Springer-Verlag, Berlin, 1982.

Simon, H., *The Science of the Artificial*. MIT Press, Cambridge, MA, 1969.

Starr, M.K., *Product Design and Decision Theory*. Prentice-Hall, Englewood Cliffs, NJ, 1963.

Suh, N.P., "Development of the Science Base for the Manufacturing Field Through the Axiomatic Approach," *Robotics and Computer Integrated Manufacturing* **1**(3/4):399–455, 1984.

Suh, N.P., Bell, A.C., and Gossard, D.C., "On an Axiomatic Approach to Manufacturing Systems," *Journal of Engineering for Industry, Transactions of A.S.M.E.* **100**(2):127–130, 1978.

Suh, N.P., Bell, A.C., Wilson, D.R., Tice, W.W., Yasuhara, M., Rinderle, J.R., and Moon, M.G., "Exploratory Study of Constraints on Design by Functional Requirements Manufacturing," Annual report 1978–79, NSF Grant DAR 77-13296, Laboratory for Manufacturing and Productivity, MIT, August 1979.

von Neumann, J., "The Mathematician: The Works of the Mind," in *Jon von Neumann's Collected Works*, Taub, A.H., ed., Vol. 1. Pergamon Press, NY, 1961.

Woodson, T.T., *Introduction to Engineering Design*. McGraw-Hill, NY, 1966.

Yoshikawa, H., "Extended General Design Theory," IFIP W.G. 5.2: *Design Theory for CAD*. North-Holland, Amsterdam, 1985.

Zwicky, F., "The Morphological Method of Analysis and Construction," *Courant*, Anniversary volume, pp. 461–470. Interscience Publishers, NY, 1948.

Problems

1.1. How many possibilities are there in a factorial design involving 270 binary variables?

1.2. Present a historical perspective on how Newton established his laws of mechanics and how they have affected the development of science and technology. (Library work is suggested.)

1.3. Thermodynamics may be considered to be a science that is based on a set of axioms. How has the development of thermodynamics axioms affected modern science and technology? (Library work is suggested.)

1.4. How should the design axioms be developed in the future to improve the practice of engineering?

1.5. Can you develop a strategy for playing a chess game by developing a set of axioms?

1.6. From the viewpoint of design axioms, which is the better form of government, the presidential form (e.g., the U.S. Government), or the parliamentary form (e.g., that of the United Kingdom)?

1.7. Identify technology-driven fields and science-driven fields (other than those given in the text). Provide your rationale.

1.8. Figure 1.4 presents a design catalogue matrix for "energy transfer for forming." It lists several different forms of energy, except "biological." Develop a means of forming the shell, using biological energy.

2

DESIGN AND DESIGN PROCESSES

2.1 Introduction

When mankind first tried to invent flying machines, people tried to imitate birds, as shown in Fig. 2.1. It would appear to most people to be a perfectly logical thing to do. After all, birds do fly, so why not create a device that looks like a bird? The FRs for this flying machine were to lift a load away from the ground against the gravitational field and move it in any desired direction. If birds can satisfy these requirements, why is that a flying machine with flapping wings does not work? Was there a fallacy in the reasoning process? This chapter examines design processes and design, in order to answer these questions as a prelude to describing the axiomatic approach.

Even a simple question related to design (such as those asked about the flying machine) cannot be answered without first understanding the nature of design, creative processes involved in design, and the role of analysis in this process. Furthermore, an endless debate could ensue from a discussion of design, because everyone has his or her own notion of design-related issues, just as he or she does about the common cold. Therefore, we must define several important terms such as design, FRs, DPs, and constraints. Although it may appear cumbersome and irrelevant to consider design in a formal and rigid framework, the short-term burden of having to deal with the formal framework may ultimately prove beneficial.

2.2 What is Design?

Design involves a continuous interplay between *what we want to achieve* and *how we want to achieve it*. For example, on a grander scale, we may say "what we want to achieve" is to go to the Moon, whereas the "how" is the physical embodiment in the form of rockets and space capsules. On a smaller scale, "what we want to achieve" may be the measurement of a minute amount of moisture in plastic pellets, and "how" may be the special titration instrument. In the case of the flapping flying machine, what people wanted was clear but how people had tried to solve the problem proved to be inadequate. These examples show that the *objective*

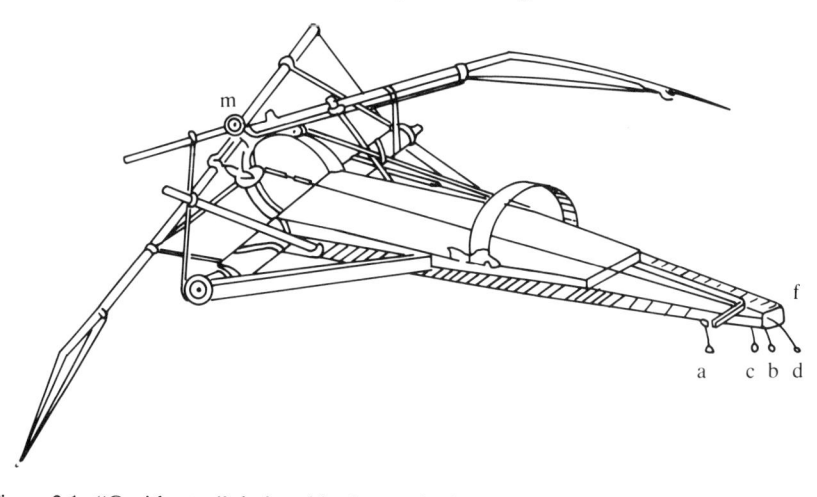

Figure 2.1. "Ornithopter" designed by Leonardo da Vinci, c. 1500. Lying prone on a board, the pilot was to operate the wings with his hands and feet by a system of pulleys. (From *Encyclopaedia Britannica*, 1966.)

of design is always stated in the *funtional domain*, whereas the *physical solution* is always generated in the *physical domain*. The design procedure involves interlinking these two domains at every hierarchical level of the design process. These two domains are inherently independent of each other. What relates these two domains is the design.

To proceed, we must determine the design's objectives by defining it in terms of specific requirements, which will be called *functional requirements*. Then, to satisfy these functional requirements, a physical embodiment characterized in terms of *design parameters* (DPs) must be created. The design process involves relating these FRs of the functional domain to the DPs of the physical domain. This is illustrated in Fig. 2.2, where DPs in the physical domain are chosen to satisfy FRs in the functional domain.

Figure 2.2. Design is defined as the mapping process from the functional space to the physical space to to satisfy the designer-specified FRs.

Design may be formally *defined* as the creation of synthesized solutions in the form of products, processes or systems that satisfy perceived needs through the *mapping* between the FRs in the functional domain and the DPs of the physical domain, through the proper *selection* of DPs that satisfy FRs. This mapping process is nonunique; therefore, more than one design may ensue from the generation of the DPs that satisfy the FRs; in other words, the actual outcome depends on a designer's individual creative process. Therefore, there can be an infinite number of plausible design solutions and mapping techniques. The design axioms provide the principles that the mapping technique must satisfy to produce a good design, and offer a basis for comparing and selecting designs.

2.3 Design Process

The design process begins with the establishment of FRs in the functional domain to satisfy a given set of needs, and ends with the creation of an entity that satisfies these FRs.

This is illustrated in Fig. 2.3, which shows that the design process begins with the recognition of a societal need. The need is formalized, resulting in a set of FRs. The selection of FRs, which defines the design problem, is left to the designer. Once the need is formalized, ideas are generated to create a product (or an organizational structure). This product is then analyzed and compared with the original set of FRs through a feedback loop. When the product does not fully satisfy the specified FRs, then one must either come up with a new idea, or change the FRs to reflect the original need more accurately. This iterative process continues until the designer produces an acceptable result.

Ultimately, the designer specifies how the transformation occurs by specifying the material, geometrical shape, physical components, and processes, as well as the spatial and temporal relationships among them. In

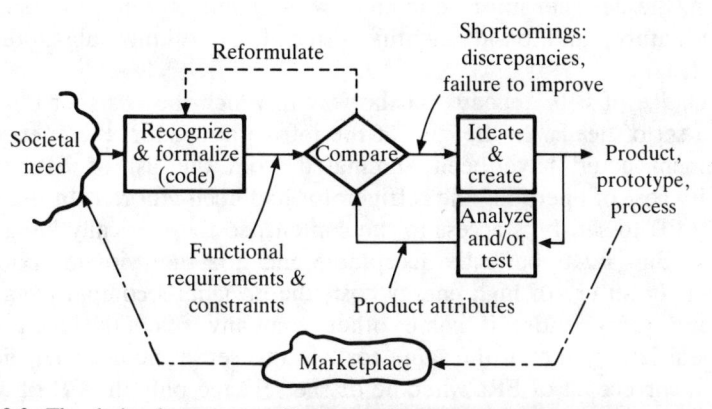

Figure 2.3. The design loop—more-effective synthesis requires enhanced creativity, more-powerful analysis, and improved decision bases. (From Wilson, 1980.)

other words, the designer creates information in the form of drawings, circuits, software, and/or equations that describe the transformation process.

There are good and not-so-good designers; one of the attributes of a good designer is the ability to satisfy the perceived needs with a minimal set of independent FRs. In the case of birds, the wing structure performs many functions: vertical take-off, cruising at an arbitrary height and speed, power for propulsion, and rapid dive. These functions are fulfilled by the bird's ability to change wingspan, wing geometry, angle of the wing with respect to the body, etc.—and birds have hollow bones, light weight, etc. When the flying-machine designers tried to imitate the birds, not only did they not know what the exact FRs were that they had to satisfy, but they also attempted to satisfy more requirements than were necessary.

As the number of FRs increases, so the solution becomes more complex. Therefore, it is necessary to satisfy only the absolutely essential functions at a given stage of design. Normally, when a problem is presented to a designer, it looks very complicated, with a large number of variables. A good designer has the ability to identify only the most important requirements and ignore those of secondary importance for consideration at a later stage. This ability requires a broad as well as an in-depth grasp of the issues involved. This ability can be cultivated, but only with great difficulty.

Furthermore, a good designer must be able to operate in the conceptual world of the functional as well as the physical domain. For example, the designer must know how to choose the FRs that are independent of each other, since two or more dependent FRs introduce unnecessary complexity without providing additional benefits. When the requirements are dependent on each other, they can be combined into one. Many designers often evolve things that cannot be manufactured, or can be manufactured only with great difficulty and expense, because they do not clearly define and analyze the relationship between DPs and FRs. In order to avoid this situation, the designer must be familiar with manufacturing processes, the laws of nature, and basic scientific principles. Nothing substitutes for knowledge.

The choice of FRs depends on the way in which the designer hopes to satisfy a set of needs. In the case of the refrigerator door, the energy loss requirement could have been eliminated from the list of FRs if the electricity cost of operating the refrigerator had been ignored. In this case, the only FR to satisfy is access to the content, so the vertically hung door shown in Fig. 1.2 is perfectly acceptable and does not violate Axiom 1. However, in an era of high energy cost, the designer's company may not sell many refrigerators if some other company offers a much more energy-efficient system at the same cost. In this sense the designer did not choose a correct set of FRs when he or she selected only the FR of access to food. The determination of a good set of FRs from diffused and often poorly defined perceived needs requires skill, sometimes extensive market

study, and many iterations. This is an important step in the design process, because the final design cannot be better than the set of FRs that it was created to satisfy.

In addition to the FRs, designers often have to specify constraints. There can be many different kinds of constraints such as cost, line voltage, geometrical size or weight, and appearance or aesthetic quality. Often these constraints have a limiting effect on design. For example, a constraint may be stated as follows: the refrigerator door should not cost more than $10 to manufacture.

Constraints differ from FRs in that, as long as the product designed does not exceed the constraints, then the solution is acceptable, whereas a specific range of design values must be maintained for each FR at all times. In other words, the resultant design must be such that constraints can be dependent both on other constraints and on FRs, whereas FRs cannot be dependent on other FRs.

2.4 Creative Process in Design

The ideational part of the design process is a creative process. How does one become creative? A number of people have tried to answer this question (Shaw, 1986). A creative person has a number of unique qualities. Such a person tends to be a risk-taker who is willing to accept failures, has a good memory and a vast store of knowledge rooted in many fields, knows how to use analogies and how to extrapolate and interpolate from known applications to a new situation, reduces a complex array of facts, data points and information to a limited number of critical sets of variables, and combines known facts to create a new solution.

To create through analogy, the person must have a multidisciplinary background. Thomas Edison made many inventions using analogical techniques (Jenkins, 1987). Charles Hall invented, from the observation that the electrolytic process can selectively deposit a material on electrodes if the material can be dissolved and ionized, the electrolytic aluminum-manufacturing method using electrochemistry. Once he got this idea, Hall's task was to look for a solvent that could dissolve aluminum oxide (alumina). Although it took many years of intensive experimentation, he finally succeeded at the age of 23 years, when he found that alumina dissolved in cryolite (a fluoride of sodium and aluminum) which could then be dissociated electrolytically to produce pure aluminum and oxygen.

Most inventive processes are hit-or-miss activities, requiring much trial and error and being an alert observer. Often people chase after worthless ideas because they do not know that their ideas have basic flaws. In the field of energy conversion, people know that their ideas are incorrect when they violate the second law of thermodynamics. When the invention involves synthesis, there was no such fundamental criterion in the past. The axioms

described in this book provide such criteria and thus can streamline the hit-or-miss process. The axioms, particularly Axiom 1, provide guidelines regarding the functions to be satisfied and the way in which they are to be satisfied. As the model shown in Fig. 1.1 indicates, the ability to analyze assists the synthesis process.

2.5 Problem Definition and FRs

In describing the design process, it was stated that the first step is the definition of the problem to be solved in terms of FRs; that is, we must establish the FRs from the needs that the final product or process must satisfy. This is clearly one of the most critical stages in the design process. This definitional step requires insight into the problem, and a knowledge base encompassing issues related to the problem. Poor problem definition leads to unacceptable or unnecessarily complex solutions.

How do we actually determine FRs to satisfy the perceived needs? There are two distinct approaches, depending on whether we are attempting to create a major new innovation or whether the goal is to improve an existing design, such as a car door. We discuss the new design case first, followed by a discussion of the second case; i.e., improvement of existing designs.

Determination of FRs in Original Design

When the goal is to create design solutions that have not previously been in existence, FRs must be defined in a *solution-neutral environment*; i.e., the functional space. Let us illustrate this point using two examples.

Example 2.1: Reduction of Materials Cost

Perceived Needs: A major instrument maker in the United States uses several million pounds of impact-grade polystyrene each year. When the company analyzed its manufacturing costs, it discovered that the materials constituted 75% of the manufacturing cost. Therefore, they asked their research and development division to devise a means of reducing the cost of materials by 20% without sacrificing the mechanical properties of the part, particularly its toughness, and the dimensions of the part. How would you deal with the problem?

Problem Definition: The problem definition in terms of FRs that can satisfy the perceived needs is straightforward.

FR_1 = Reduce the material cost by 20%.
FR_2 = Maintain toughness of the plastic part to equal or exceed that of the original part made of impact-grade polystyrene.
Constraint = The overall manufacturing cost must be less than the current cost.

These FRs and the constraint are defined purely in the functional domain. We have not yet thought about how we are going to satisfy them in the physical domain. That is, the FRs are defined without any preconceived notion of a physical solution in mind.

Choice of DPs: Having defined FRs, we can now choose DPs to satisfy the FRs by conceiving a physical solution in the physical domain. It is clear that one way of reducing cost is by filling (and thus replacing) impact-grade polystyrene with an inexpensive filler. However, most fillers are so big they reduce the toughness of the plastic by allowing cracks to propagate from these filler sites. Furthermore, even if very small, uniform fillers were available, it would be impossible to disperse them in the polymer, because they tend to agglomerate.

One possible design solution is to introduce microvoids whose dimensions are smaller than the critical flaw size in the polystyrene, so they cannot act as crack-initiation sites. Microvoids could act as crack arresters or crack-tip blunters, or perhaps as a crazing initiation site, any of which would produce a material that is tougher than the original material. For this design solution, the DPs may be written as

DP_1 = Volume fraction of microvoids.

DP_2 = Characteristic dimension of the microvoids.

Having defined FRs and DPs, the product is now designed. The next task calls for the analysis of the proposed design solution to see whether it violates the laws of nature and the design axioms. FR_1 is satisfied by DP_1 and DP_1 only, whereas FR_2 is satisfied by DP_2 and DP_2 only. Therefore, Axiom 1 is satisfied.

Once we know that we have a product that satisfies the original set of FRs by controlling the volume fraction of voids and the dimension of the voids, we have to design a process that can produce the product. Such a process was eventually developed, as discussed in greater detail in Chapter 6. This product is now known worldwide as the *microcellular plastic*.

Example 2.2: "Lessons of *Sunraycer*" (adapted from Wilson et al., 1989)

Perceived Needs: Hans Tholstrup, an Australian adventurer and visionary, and outspoken advocate for fuel conservation, energy renewal, and reduced air pollution, conceived the idea for a race across Australia of cars powered by solar energy. *Sunraycer*, designed and built by a team of engineers led by Paul MacCready and engineers from Hughes Aircraft Co., General Motors Corporation, and AeroVironment Inc., won the 1,867-mile Pentax World Solar Challenge race. MacCready and his associates defined FRs based around the challenge posed by Tholstrup: win the race with a solar powered vehicle. The constraints (i.e., race rules) stipulated that the vehicle had to fit within a volume 6 m long, 2 m wide and 2 m high, with a minimum height of 1 m.

Problem Definition: MacCready and his associates used four FRs at the highest level of the design process: *simplicity, efficiency, light weight,* and *reliability*. These four FRs were defined in "solution-neutral" environment. The difference between their approach and others is obvious from their statements:

"Most of the competitors sought to maximize power output with solar panels that tilted to track the Sun or with large, fixed side and top panels that were mounted on the car bodies. These panels increased aerodynamic drag because of the increased height of the vehicle, the large exposed surfaces and the flow interference between the panels and the car body. They also tended to be vulnerable to crosswinds, and their greater mechanical complexity made them heavier and less reliable."

"In developing *Sunraycer*, we tried to avoid preconceived notions about what might work best. Instead we designed for *simplicity, efficiency, light weight,* and *reliability.*"

Final Design: Once they defined the FRs, they could begin to conceive the physical solutions, which they evaluated over a short period. "In the initial three-week planning stage, begun in March of 1987, we quickly considered the trade-offs involved in a dozen different configurations of solar-panel shape and orientation, body contour, and the location, number, and structural support of the wheels. (We explored almost every vehicle configuration that finally showed up at Darwin.)" Once they decided on the design solution at the highest level of the FR hierarchy, they could then proceed with the establishment of the low-level FRs.

Their final design is illustrated in Fig. 2.4.

In Examples 2.1 and 2.2, the perceived needs were directly translated into a set of FRs in a solution-neutral environment. However, in many cases the establishment of an acceptable (or correct) set of FRs may require an iterative process. The iteration may involve the entire life cycle of product development, including the complete sequence of design–manufacture–testing–use, which is time-consuming and costly, both financially and in terms of lost opportunity.

The most desirable iteration cycle, next to "no iteration," is the reiteration at the conceptual stage of the design process itself. Once the conceptual design is completed, the expected performance of the resultant design product can be compared with the original perceived needs of the product. If they differ, then an improved set of FRs can be established without incurring the cost of making and testing the hardware and/or software. In some case a prototype hardware cannot actually be made because it is so costly (e.g., nuclear power plants, large bridges, and manufacturing plants).

One of the major problems in design is that designers do not state explicitly the FRs that their design must satisfy. They try to design intuitively. They also do not recognize the probable need to reiterate the establishment of FRs until a satisfactory design results. When a new set of FRs are established, the corresponding solution may be completely different from those previously tried.

It may be useful to state once more the importance of proper problem definition in design: the perceived needs must be reduced to an imaginative set of FRs as the first and most critical stage of the design process. In the absence of a proper set of FRs, a good design is not likely to result.

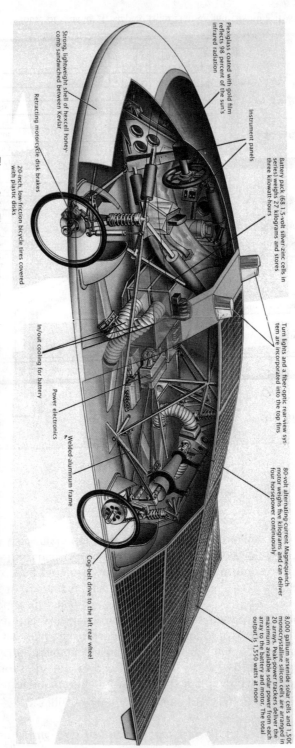

Plexiglass coated with gold film reflects 98 percent of the sun's infrared radiation

Strong, lightweight shell of hexcell honeycomb sandwiched between Kevlar

Retracting motorcycle disk brakes

20-inch, low-friction bicycle tires covered with plastic disks

instrument panels

Battery pack (68 1.5-volt silver-zinc cells in series) weighs 27 kilograms and stores three kilowatt-hours

Turn lights and a fiber-optic rear-view system are incorporated into the top fins

In/out cooling for battery

Power electronics

Welded-aluminum frame

Cog-belt drive to the left rear wheel

80-volt alternating-current Magnequench motor weighs five kilograms and can deliver four horsepower continuously maximum available solar power from each

8,000 gallium arsenide solar cells and 1,500 monocrystalline silicon cells are arranged in 20 arrays. Peak-power trackers deliver the maximum available solar power from each array to the battery and motor. The total output is 1,550 watts at noon

Figure 2.4. Final design for *Sunraycer*. (From Wilson et al., 1989; courtesy of Scientific American.)

Determination of the FRs for Improvement of Existing Design

Examples 2.1 and 2.2 illustrated how and why FRs should be established in a solution-neutral environment, without being biased by preconceived physical solutions. In the case of Example 2.1, if we had attempted to modify an existing foamed plastic processing technique, then it is highly probable that we would have defined a wrong set of FRs. In Example 2.2 it is obvious that the vehicles whose design was biased by preconceived physical embodiment failed to win the race.

In contrast to these examples, there are cases where the goal is to improve an existing design by incorporating the "customer attributes" in FRs. One of the concepts advanced to define a set of FRs from the attributes that consumers demand is the "House of Quality" (Hauser and

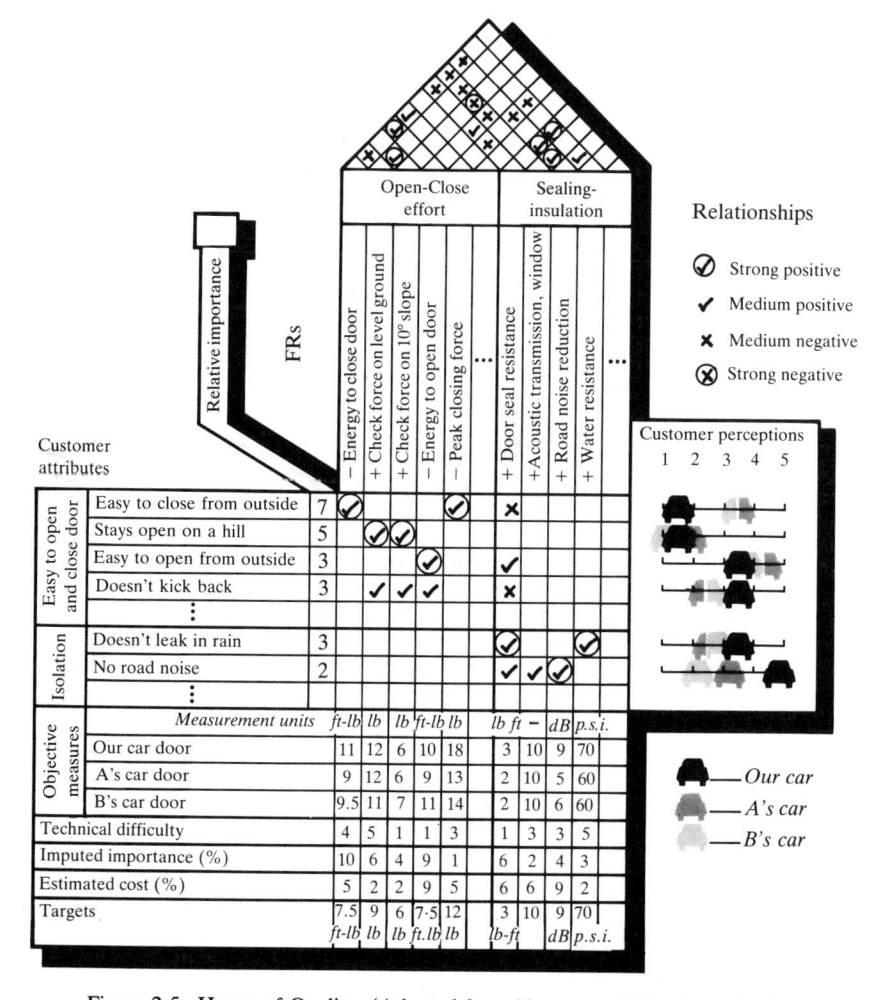

Figure 2.5. House of Quality. (Adapted from Hauser and Clausing, 1988.)